W9-BSV-871

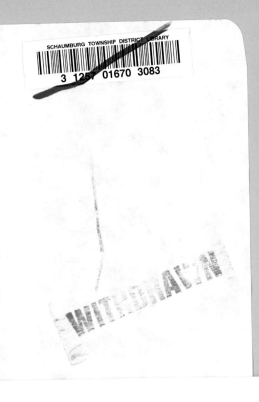

The complete book of
hot & spicy
asian cooking

VICKI LILEY

PERIPLUS EDITIONS
Singapore • Hong Kong • Indonesia

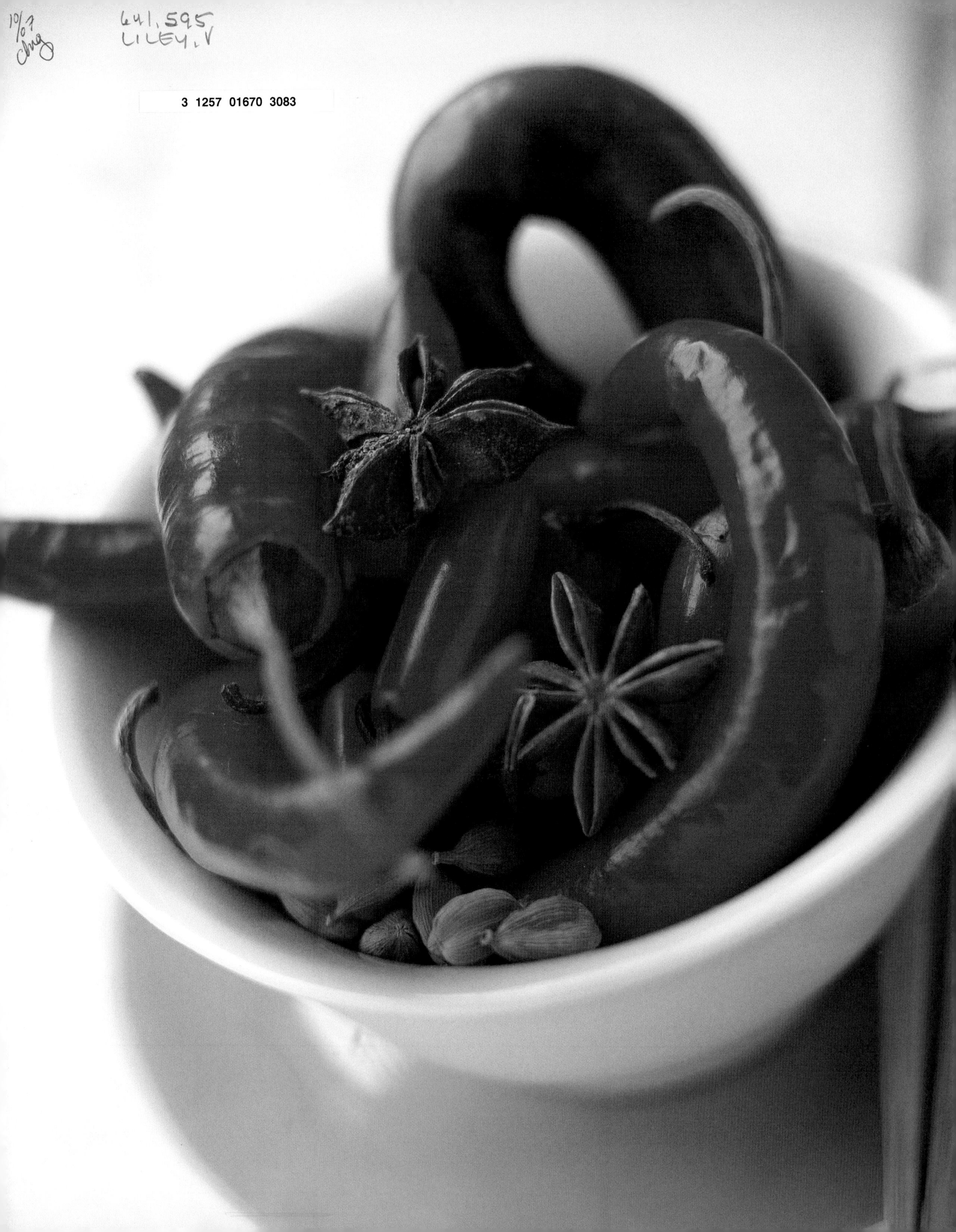

Contents

Recipe list

Introduction

The most common misconception about hot and spicy food is that there is a single ingredient that makes the dish extremely hot. Hot and spicy meals are so much more than one element, and they vary in flavor as they do in color. It is the combination of the ingredients, the herbs and spices as well as the meat and vegetables, that creates the taste sensations.

Nothing embodies the mysteries of cooking quite like the herbs and spices used. They are as versatile as they are special and they are as varied as the dialects of the world. When it comes to taste, spices provide an endless variety of possibility. Originally, spices were used as a preservative and for their medicinal properties. Today, they are used mainly for flavoring and to make food more attractive by providing color. Turmeric, which makes food yellow, is used to color rice and white vegetables such as cauliflower and potato. Coriander leaves and green chilies define Thailand's famous green curries, while red spices give dishes a vivid colour and a sharp, pungent flavor.

Hot and spicy meals needn't be excruciatingly hot either. The chilies, herbs and spices used in this book can be added, subtracted or substituted to suit individual tastes. Whether you are a lover of hot, fiery flavors or of more subtle, tangy aromas, you will find a suitable recipe. There is a vast array of recipes including appetizers and dips, seafood, meat and vegetable dishes, and delicious sauces.

Cold water is the most authentic beverage to drink with a hot and spicy meal, because many fizzy or carbonated drinks, including beer, tend to exaggerate the burning sensation of a hot spice. Surprisingly, so does iced water. Lovers of hot and spicy foods will be impressed with the drinks and desserts we've included to help cool the fire in the belly during and after a meal.

An important aim of this book is to show just how easy it is to prepare and cook traditional hot and spicy foods. For instance, spices were once ground on a flat, rectangular stone with a stone rolling pin. In places such as India, it's still common to see spice-grinders standing on street corners pounding spices in giant mortars, throwing the heavy pestle with skill and ease, making passersby sneeze as the finely powdered spices fly into the hot air. For that ultimate authentic touch, a more manageable kitchen-sized mortar and pestle set will produce as genuine a result in your own home, or you can reach for a blender or an unemployed coffee grinder to do the job. In the next few pages you'll find even more hints on how to prepare chilies, herbs and spices.

We have researched far and wide to provide a selection of the many styles of hot and spicy recipes from Thailand, Sri Lanka, India, Burma and Indonesia, among many other countries. When it comes to taste, hot and spicy foods contain an endless variety of possibilities. We hope you enjoy the ingenious ways people throughout the world have incorporated local and imported ingredients to make some of the world's tastiest and best-loved meals—hot and spicy.

Chilies

The chilies most commonly used are small, red, hot chilies, and the longer, milder red and green chilies. Generally, the rule of thumb is the smaller the chili, the more fiery it tastes. Color, however, is not a reliable indication of a chili's pungency, with small green chilies sometimes more pungent than red ones.

Many people find chili an intimidating food both to handle and to consume. The volatile oils in a fresh chili can burn the skin on contact (see page 16 for step-by-step preparation). Therefore it is wise to wear disposable plastic gloves when handling chilies and always wash your hands well with soap afterward. If you eat a chili dish that is too hot, consuming bread, rice, yogurt or milk will help tame the heat. Do not drink beer or sparkling drinks.

The recipes in this book call for chilies in amounts that may seem daunting. If you are unaccustomed to cooking with chili, you may want to use fewer chilies than called for in a recipe and gradually raise your tolerance level. The membrane and seeds are the hottest parts—for making sambals, the whole chili is used, seeds and all, and they are generally ground or pureed in a blender (such as the Indonesian sambal oelek). The heat or bite of a chili can be reduced by removing its seeds and white membrane. You can also achieve a milder flavor by adding chilies to a dish during cooking, then lifting them out and discarding them before serving. Remember, it's good etiquette to warn your guests that a dish you're serving contains chilies. But if you want the authentic fiery quality of various Asian cuisines, prepare the recipes as directed, using the full amount of fresh chilies.

Dried chilies are safe enough to handle until they have been soaked and ground, after which you should remember to wash your hands at once. If frying dried chilies as an accompaniment to a meal, use them whole, dropping them straight into hot oil. If they are being soaked and ground for a sauce or curry, first break or snip off the stalk end and shake to loosen and discard the seeds. Though dried chilies contribute plenty of heat and flavor to a dish, they do not have as severe an effect on the skin as fresh chilies.

When buying, fresh chilies should be firm, glossy and evenly colored. Avoid chilies that are musty, soft or bruised. The best way to store fresh chili is to wrap them well in paper towels, then place them in a plastic bag. They can be stored in the refrigerator for up to a week. Purchase dried chilies in small amounts and keep them in a cool dry place. Use them as soon as possible for optimum flavor.

Of the nearly 200 varieties of fresh chilies found around the world, many are available for use by the home cook. Following is a guide to some of the most common varieties. For the purposes of this book, we have rated them on a scale of three stars, from mild (one star) to medium (two stars) to hot (three stars).

Bird's eye

Used in Thai cooking, bird's eye chilies are blazing hot, with a clear, fiery taste. These small green or red chilies, about ½ inch (12 mm) long, should be used in small quantities. Heat rating: ***

Habanero

Considerable heat is packed into this small chili, one of the hottest used in cooking. The habanero, measuring about 2 inches (5 cm) long and about as wide, varies from green to orange or red when ripe. Heat rating: ***

Jalapeño

Popular and widely available, this Mexican chili, about 2 inches (5 cm) long, has thick flesh and delivers moderate heat. Green and ripe red chilies are sold in most markets. Heat rating: **

Serrano

This widely available, green or red chili has thick flesh and a strong, pronounced heat. Slim and tapered, it reaches 2 inches (5 cm) long. Heat rating: ***

Thai green

A medium–hot chili, also known as Thai dragon, it grows up to 1½ inches (4 cm) long. The somewhat milder, green Anaheim chili, similarly shaped and up to 6 inches (15 cm) long, may be substituted. Heat rating: **

Thai red

The ripe counterpart to the Thai green chili, this chili is also medium–hot and up to 1½ inches (4 cm) long. The red Anaheim chili or the red Dutch chili may be used in its place. Heat rating: **

Dried red chilies

Sold in Asian stores in bags or packets, these can be large or small red chilies which have been dried.

Chili powder

This is available in bottles or you can grind your own using small, dried red chilies or red chili flakes.

Chili flakes

Available in bottles or you can make your own by coarsely crushing small, dried red chilies.

Chili oil

This spicy oil is produced by steeping red chilies in oil. It is available bottled or you can prepare your own (see page 220 for recipe).

Sambal oelek

An Indonesian paste that consists of ground chili combined with salt and occasionally vinegar. This spicy condiment is available bottled, or you can prepare your own (see page 228 for recipe).

Preparing fresh chilies

Take special care not to touch your face or eyes when handling chilies, and always wash your hands thoroughly with soap and hot water afterward. To protect your hands from a chili's heat, you can wear disposable gloves.

1 Using a sharp knife, trim the stem from the chili.

2 Cut the chili in half lengthwise.

3 Scrape the seeds and the white pith (membrane) from the skin. (Some recipes require the seeds to be used for a hotter flavor so skip this step if this is the case.)

4 Slice or chop the chili as required.

Preparing dried chilies

It is best to wear disposable gloves when handling any chili. When soaking dried chili be careful not to let the soaking liquid touch your hands as it could burn your skin.

1 Pull or cut the stem off the long chilies.

2 Roll the chili pod gently in the palm of your hand.

3 Turn the chili upside down and shake out the loosened seeds.

4 Soak pods in warm water for 10 minutes, then drain.

Herbs and spices

Today's cook can make superb use of an extensive array of fresh and dried herbs and spices, and other seasonings. From fresh cilantro (fresh coriander), galangal and ginger to saffron, cardamom, and cumin seeds, these seasonings are combined to give each dish a characteristic complexity and appealing richness. The secret to using herbs and spices is not so much matching them to the vegetable or meat, but learning how to combine them in order to achieve a range of subtle, strong, tangy, and always interesting flavors.

You may have a green thumb and grow and dry your own herbs. A few hints for those who don't, purchase fresh herbs and spices for immediate use. You can store them in a plastic bag in the refrigerator, but only for a short time. When buying dried spices, it's better to buy in small quantities and store in a cool, dark place and use as soon as possible for best results. Correctly dried herbs always taste stronger than the fresh versions, as only the watery content has evaporated, leaving a concentration of essential oils. Whole dried leaves, or chopped or crumbled dried leaves, are more powerful in fragrance and taste than powdered herbs, which often include ground stalks as well.

Each culture's culinary style seems to favor specific herbs and spices. Basil, garlic, and chili are a popular combination for Thai cooking. The Vietnamese love garlic and coriander. The Chinese prefer a subtle blending of sweet and sour, hence the use of lemongrass, ginger, and star anise. The opportunities to create new flavors using herbs and spices are endless: there's a whole world of flavors to explore. Most importantly, each combination can be adapted to suit your personal taste. Here are some of the more popular ones we use in this book, but don't forget to look at the glossary for more choices.

Bay leaves

Dried leaves from a tree belonging to the laurel family. The leaves impart a lemon nutmeg flavor. They are used in cooking, but are not edible.

Betel leaves

Thick, smooth and dark in color, these edible leaves are used mainly to wrap foods and they vary in size.

Cardamom

This member of the ginger family produces pods that contain seeds with a strong lemony flavor. It is available ground.

Cilantro

Pungent, fragrant leaves from the coriander plant, resembling parsley and also called Chinese parsley and fresh coriander. They have a sharp, tangy, fresh flavor and aroma. The leaves, stems, and roots are all essential seasonings in Asian cooking.

Cinnamon sticks

Rolled pieces of the inner bark of the branches of a small evergreen tree native to Sri Lanka and India. It has a distinctive sweet flavor and aroma, and is available ground.

Cloves

The dried unopened flower buds of a tropical evergreen tree, these have an extremely pungent sweet taste and aroma. Available whole or ground.

Coriander seeds

Tiny yellow-tan seeds from the cilantro (fresh coriander) plant. Used, whole or ground, as a spice, its flavor is reminiscent of lemon, sage and caraway.

Cumin seeds

Dried, small, crescent-shaped seeds from a plant related to parsley. Available whole or ground, and in three colors: amber, white and black. They have a powerful earthy, nutty flavor and aroma. Briefly dry-roasting them will bring out their earthy, pungent and slightly bitter flavor.

Curry leaves

Bright, shiny leaves used in Indian and Southeast Asian cuisines. Added to sauces, curries, and stir-fries, they impart a subtle curry flavor to the food.

Galangal

A rhizome with a sharp flavor, sometimes called Thai ginger, it has reddish skin, orange or white flesh and a peppery gingerlike flavor. Fresh galangal should be peeled before use, then sliced or grated. It is also available dried.

Ginger

Thick rootlike rhizome of the ginger plant, a tall flowering tropical plant native to China. It has a sharp pungent flavor. Once the tan skin is peeled from fresh ginger, the ivory to greenish yellow flesh is grated or sliced. Used fresh in sweet and savory cooking and beverages.

Green peppercorns

Unripened peppercorns with a soft texture and a fresh sour flavor. Available freeze-dried or pickled in brine or vinegar. Refrigerate after opening.

Kaffir lime leaves

Fragrant, shiny dark green leaves from the kaffir lime tree, used fresh or dried, whole or shredded, for their enticing citrus flavor.

Lemongrass

Pale stalks of a tropical grass that contribute an intense lemon flavor to Southeast Asian dishes. After the green blades are removed, the stalks are bruised or sliced before use.

Mustard seeds

Seeds from a plant belonging to the cabbage family. Available in yellow, brown or black.

Saffron threads

Saffron threads are the dried stigmas from a variety of crocus flower, each of which produces only three stigmas. Harvesting saffron is labor-intensive, making it the most costly spice in the world. Saffron threads are generally soaked in a warm liquid to release their intense gold-yellow color and pungent, earthy aroma and flavor.

Sesame seeds

The seeds of an herb that is grown in India and other parts of Asia. Whole or ground white sesame seeds are used in savory dishes, breads and many sweets. Sometimes the seeds are toasted to add a nuttier flavor.

Star anise

Dark brown star-shaped spice with a flavor similar to aniseed but with more depth and sweetness. It is the dried fruit from a variety of evergreen magnolia tree. Commonly used in Chinese cooking, star anise also makes an appearance in Indian foods.

Tamarind

Tamarind pods contain small seeds and a sour-sweet pulp that, when dried, becomes extremely sour. The paste, sold in block form, requires dilution in hot water and straining. More convenient is commercially available tamarind pulp, puree or water, sold in jars.

Thai basil

Also known as holy basil, this variety of the popular herb has a strong, distinctive flavor.

Turmeric

Like galangal and ginger, fresh turmeric is a rhizome that grows underground. Its flavor is more pronounced than turmeric powder.

Vietnamese mint

Spicy hot, this variety of mint makes a delicious addition to Asian salads.

Toasting spices and seeds

Because spices and seeds toast at different times, toast them separately. The general rule is to use your nose: once fragrant, remove from heat immediately. Do not overcook or they may become bitter or acrid.

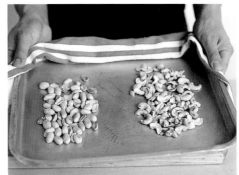

1 Place spice or seeds in a dry wok or frying pan over medium heat, and toast, stirring constantly, until lightly golden and fragrant.

2 Alternatively, preheat the oven to 400°F (200°C/Gas 6). Spread the nuts or seeds on a rimmed baking pan and toast for 8–12 minutes, shaking the pan once to ensure even browning.

3 If spices need grinding, let cool then grind in a mortar.

Preparing steamed rice

Though commonly referred to as "steamed rice," standard rice that accompanies most hot and spicy food is actually boiled. When cooked, rice swells to two and a half times its volume. Estimate about 1–1½ cups cooked rice per person.

1 Rinse rice until the water runs clear, but do not overwork the rice or the grains may break. Drain the rice and put it in a deep, heavy saucepan with a tight-fitting lid.

2 Fill the pan with water to cover the rice by ¾ inch (2 cm). Traditionally, cooks measured by placing their index finger on the rice, adding just enough water to touch their first joint. Measure the water from the top of the rice.

3 Over high heat, bring the water to a boil and cook until craters form on the rice's surface and the water has disappeared. Immediately cover tightly and reduce heat to a bare simmer. Cook until tender; about 20 minutes. Do not lift the lid during cooking.

4 Use a wooden rice paddle or wooden spoon to fluff the rice up and loosen the grains. If cooking in a nonstick pan, using a bamboo or wooden implement avoids scratching the surface.

Cooking noodles

Noodles come in an endless array of shapes, sizes and varieties. Always check the package for cooking times and serving ideas. Use the following cooking times as a guide and always check the noodles during cooking by tasting a strand. Noodles for soups should be slightly undercooked, so they don't fall apart. Noodles for most other dishes should be cooked through. There are basically two ways to cook noodles:

1 Place noodles in a heatproof bowl and cover with boiling water. Soak noodles until soft, then drain. This method is suitable only for fine noodles such as cellophane (bean thread) noodles, rice vermicelli and thin egg noodles.

2 Bring a large saucepan of water to the boil, add noodles and cook until tender, then drain. This method is suitable for all noodles.

Cellophane noodles Fine white cellophane noodles need only be softened in boiling water for 10 minutes; they do not require boiling. Or for a crisp texture, deep-fry them in hot oil until golden and crisp, 1 minute or less.

Egg noodles If fresh, cook in boiling water for about 3 minutes. If dried, cook in boiling water for about 5 minutes. Some precooked fresh egg noodles need only be soaked in hot water for 8–10 minutes; check package for directions.

Hokkien noodles Cook in boiling water for 3–4 minutes or stir-fry in hot oil for 3–4 minutes. Some varieties are precooked; check package for directions.

Ramen noodles Cook in boiling water for about 5 minutes.

Rice stick noodles Soften dried noodles in hot water for 15 minutes or cook in boiling water for 2–3 minutes. Stir-fry fresh noodles for 2–3 minutes. Some thin rice stick noodles only require soaking in boiling water before adding to soups or stir-fries. Rice vermicelli can be deep-fried to create a crisp "bird's nest" for serving stir-fry dishes.

Soba noodles
Fresh: Cook in boiling water for about 1½ minutes. Dried: Cook in boiling water for 5–6 minutes.

Somen noodles Cook in boiling water for about 3 minutes.

Spring roll wrappers Steam filled wrappers for 5 minutes or deep-fry in hot oil until golden and crisp.

Udon noodles If fresh, cook in boiling water for about 2½ minutes. If dried, cook in boiling water for 10–12 minutes.

Wheat flour noodles If fresh, cook in boiling water for 3 minutes. If dried, cook in boiling water for 4–5 minutes.

Wonton wrappers White (wheat flour) wrappers should be cooked in boiling water or steam filled wrappers for about 6 minutes; deep-fry until golden and crisp. Yellow (egg dough) ones can be cooked in boiling water for about 4 minutes; deep-fry until golden and crisp.

appetizers and dips

Chili herb shrimp

Serves 10

⅓ cup (3 fl oz/90 ml) olive oil

2 tablespoons peeled and chopped fresh ginger

2 garlic cloves, crushed

2 small pieces lemongrass, crushed

1 small red chili, seeded and chopped

2 limes or lemons, juiced

¼ cup (⅓ oz/10 g) chopped mixed fresh herbs of
    choice

4 lb (2 kg) jumbo shrimp (green king prawns), peeled
    and deveined

2 tablespoons olive oil, for cooking

20 short bamboo or metal skewers

lime or lemon wedges, for garnish

In a large bowl, combine ⅓ cup olive oil, ginger, garlic, lemongrass, chili, lime juice and herbs. Mix well. Add shrimp and toss until well coated in marinade. Cover with plastic wrap and refrigerate for 1 hour.

In a frying pan over medium heat, warm 2 tablespoons oil. Drain shrimp. Working in batches, fry shrimp until they just change color, 2–3 minutes.

Thread shrimp onto skewers and serve with lime or lemon wedges.

Chili noodle crab cakes

Makes 8 cakes

4 oz (125 g) cellophane (bean thread) noodles

vegetable oil as needed

8 large fresh basil leaves

6 oz (180 g) fresh or canned crabmeat

1/3 cup (3 fl oz/80 ml) coconut milk

1 tablespoon red curry paste (see page 27)

2 eggs, beaten

1 tablespoon fish sauce

2 tablespoons chopped fresh cilantro (fresh
   coriander)

2 teaspoons lime juice

Thai sweet chili sauce

1 small red chili, seeded if desired, and sliced
   (optional)

Soak noodles in boiling water for 10 minutes. Drain and pat dry with paper towels.

Preheat oven to 350°F (180°C/Gas 4).

Brush 8 cups of standard muffin pan with oil. Place basil leaf in each muffin cup. Line cups with noodles, dividing evenly.

In a bowl, combine crabmeat, coconut milk, curry paste, eggs, fish sauce, cilantro and lime juice. Mix well. Pour over noodles.

Bake cakes until firm to touch, 15–20 minutes. Remove from oven and allow to cool in pan.

Remove from pan and serve warm with Thai sweet chili sauce. Garnish with chili slices, if desired.

Corn and shrimp cakes

Serves 6

6 garlic cloves
5 sprigs fresh cilantro (fresh coriander)
¼ teaspoon red chili flakes
¼ teaspoon sugar
2 tablespoons fish sauce
2 cups (8 oz/250 g) fresh or frozen corn
5 oz (150 g) shrimp (prawns), shelled, deveined and
  coarsely chopped
2 tablespoons cornflour
2 eggs, lightly beaten
½ cup (4 fl oz/125 ml) vegetable oil
sriracha sauce (see pork patties, page 36)

In a food processor, process the garlic, cilantro, chili flakes, sugar and fish sauce to a paste in a food processor. Scrape into a mixing bowl.

Place the corn kernels in the processor and pulse once to chop coarsely. Add to bowl with seasoning paste. Add shrimp. Sprinkle mixture with cornflour and stir through. Add eggs to bowl and mix well.

Heat the oil in a wok. Drop corn mixture by rounded tablespoonfuls into hot oil and fry until brown, turning once. Drain on paper towels.

Serve hot with sriracha sauce.

Curried mango dip

Serves 4–6

1 tablespoon vegetable oil

1 onion, finely chopped

1 teaspoon mild curry powder

10 oz (300 g) plain (natural) yogurt

2 tablespoons mango chutney

mixed fresh vegetables and baby pappadams, for
  serving

In a small frying pan over medium heat, heat oil. Add onion and cook until softened, about 1 minute. Stir in curry powder and cook until aromatic, about 1 minute.

Remove pan from heat and allow to cool. Gently stir in yogurt and mango chutney.

Spoon into a serving bowl, place in center of a platter and surround with vegetables such as Belgian endive (chicory) leaves, slices of carrot, celery, red and green bell peppers (capsicums), English (hothouse) cucumber, blanched cauliflower florets and blanched asparagus spears.

If desired, fry pappadams in hot vegetable oil or microwave on High according to directions on package.

Curried mixed nuts

Makes 3 cups (15 oz/470 g)

3 tablespoons vegetable oil

1 cup (5 oz/150 g) cashew nuts

1 cup (5 oz/150 g) blanched whole almonds

1 cup (5 oz/150 g) raw peanuts

1 tablespoon sea salt

1 teaspoon garam masala (see page 223)

½ teaspoon chili powder

In a wok or skillet, heat oil over medium heat. Add cashews and cook, stirring constantly, until lightly browned, 1–2 minutes. Using a slotted spoon, transfer to paper towels to drain. Repeat to fry almonds, then peanuts. Combine nuts in a medium bowl. Add remaining ingredients and stir until well combined. Serve at room temperature.

Tip

These tasty little morsels make a great snack to serve with drinks.

Curry Puffs

Makes about 20

2 tablespoons vegetable oil or ghee

1 medium onion, chopped very finely

½ lb (250 g) ground (minced) beef or lamb

½-inch (1.5-cm) piece fresh ginger, chopped very
   finely

1 cup (6 oz/180 g) diced cooked potato

½ cup (1 ½ ox/45 g) cooked green peas

½ cup (2 oz/60 g) cooked diced carrots

1 tablespoon curry powder or 2 teaspoons garam
   masala (see page 223)

1 tablespoon finely chopped fresh cilantro
   (fresh coriander) or mint

1½ teaspoons salt

½ teaspoon black pepper

4–5 tablespoons water

1 pack frozen puff pastry, thawed

1 beaten egg

cayenne or paprika

Sauté onion until lightly browned. Add meat and ginger
and sauté until meat changes color, but do not brown.
Add vegetables and curry powder and cook for
1 minute, stirring continually. Add herbs, seasonings
and water and simmer, uncovered, until liquid has
completely evaporated.

Preheat an oven to 360°F (180°C/Gas 4). Sprinkle flour
lightly over a board. Roll pastry thinly and cut into
3-inch (8-cm) rounds. Place a portion of filling in middle
of each round. Moisten edges with beaten egg, fold
over and press edges together. Press points of a fork
on edges to seal and decorate.

Brush top surface of each curry puff lightly with beaten
egg and sprinkle with cayenne or paprika. Place on a
baking sheet or cookie tray and bake until golden
brown; about 18 minutes. Allow to cool for 2 minutes
on tray, then serve.

Fried prawn cakes with chili-lime sauce

Serves 4–6

1½ lb (750 g) shrimp (prawns), peeled and deveined

1 handful fresh cilantro (fresh coriander) sprigs with
    roots

6 garlic cloves, peeled

½ teaspoon black pepper

2 serrano chilies, stemmed

½ teaspoon salt or to taste

3 tablespoons to ¾ cup (6 fl oz/175 ml) vegetable oil

For chili-lime sauce

6 red chilies, stemmed and finely sliced

4 garlic cloves, finely chopped

½ cup (4 fl oz/125 ml) fresh lime juice

3 tablespoons fish sauce

In a food processor, combine all the ingredients except oil and chili-lime sauce and process to a paste. Wet hands and form mixture into walnut-sized balls, then flatten into patties.

In a wok or frying pan, heat oil and fry patties in batches (avoid overcrowding), turning once, until brown. Drain on paper towels.

To make chili-lime sauce: Combine all ingredients in a glass or ceramic bowl and mix well.

Serve patties warm with sauce.

Tip

Chili-lime sauce is a wonderful dipping sauce for roasted or barbecued meats and fish. It does not keep, so make it fresh each time you use it.

In a bowl, combine all ingredients except piper leaves. Use your hands to knead well, for about 3 minutes. Meanwhile, soak 60 wooden toothpicks in water for a few minutes to prevent charring.

Place a piper leaf, dark side down, on a work surface. Place about 1 tablespoon filling in middle of leaf and roll into a tiny cylinder about 2 inches (5 cm) long and ³/₄ inch (2 cm) thick. Make sure the meat is fully covered by the leaf, although covering the two ends is optional. Skewer with a toothpick. Continue with remaining meat and leaves.

Prepare a charcoal grill (barbecue) or preheat an oven broiler (grill) with the grilling rack set about 5 inches (12 cm) from heat source. Cook parcels, turning twice, until cooked through, about 8–10 minutes. Watch carefully, as they tend to char quickly.

Serve with nuoc cham nem sauce.

Tips

• If ground sirloin is unavailable, use regular ground (minced) stewing steak (chuck or hamburger), as it has more flavor than lean ground round (topside). The fat content in ground beef produces a more tender product, as the melting fat bastes the patties internally during cooking.

• If piper leaves are unavailable, use cured grape leaves. Alternatively, use aluminum foil.

Grilled beef
wrapped in leaves

Makes about 60

4 oz (125 g) fresh pork fatback, ground (minced) or
   finely diced
1 lb (500 g) ground (minced) beef, e.g. sirloin (rump)
¹/₄ cup (³/₄ oz/20 g) finely chopped brown or pink
   shallots (French shallots)
3 large cloves garlic, finely chopped
1 fresh small red chili, seeded and finely chopped
2 tablespoons fish sauce
1 tablespoon sugar
1 teaspoon salt
1 teaspoon ground pepper
juice of 1 lemon
about 60 piper leaves
nuoc cham nem sauce (see page 225)

Hot-and-spicy money bags

Makes 20

6 Chinese dried mushrooms

4 oz (125 g) jumbo shrimp (green king prawns), peeled, deveined and finely chopped

12½ oz (375 g) ground (minced) pork

1 or 2 small red chilies, seeded, if desired, and finely chopped

⅓ cup (½ oz/15 g) chopped fresh cilantro (fresh coriander)

6 scallions (shallots/spring onions), finely chopped

2 cloves garlic, finely chopped

3 teaspoons peeled and grated fresh ginger

2 teaspoons Asian sesame oil

3 teaspoons soy sauce

2 teaspoons rice wine

20 square wonton wrappers

4 cups (32 fl oz/1 L) vegetable oil, for deep-frying

soy sauce, for dipping

Place mushrooms in a small bowl, add boiling water to cover and let stand until softened, 10–15 minutes. Drain and squeeze excess liquid from mushrooms. Finely chop, discarding thick stems. In a bowl, combine mushrooms, shrimp, pork, chili, cilantro, scallions, garlic, ginger, sesame oil, soy sauce and rice wine. Using wet hands, mix until well combined.

Place wonton wrappers on a work surface and keep covered with a damp kitchen towel to prevent drying. Working with one wonton wrapper at a time, lay it on work surface and place 1 teaspoon filling in middle. Brush edges with water. Gather edges and twist to seal. Repeat with remaining wrappers and filling.

In a large wok, heat oil until it reaches 375°F (190°C) on a deep-frying thermometer or until a small bread cube dropped in oil sizzles and turns golden. Working in batches, add wontons and fry until golden, 1–2 minutes. Using a slotted spoon, remove from hot oil and drain on paper towels. Serve hot with soy sauce for dipping.

Massaman curry bites

Makes 12

2 tablespoons Massaman Curry Paste (see page 226)
2$\frac{1}{2}$ oz (75 g) white-fleshed fish, ground (minced)
2$\frac{1}{2}$ oz (75 g) firm or extra-firm tofu, drained and
  shredded
$\frac{1}{3}$ cup ($\frac{2}{3}$ oz/20 g) soybean sprouts, blanched and
  finely chopped
2 scallions (shallots/spring onions), finely chopped
1 tablespoon coconut milk
12 large deep-fried tofu puffs (about 5 oz/150 g)
$\frac{1}{4}$ cup (2 fl oz/60 ml) ketjap manis mixed with
  1 tablespoon light soy sauce

Preheat oven to 400°F (200°C/Gas 6).

In a medium bowl, combine curry paste, fish, shredded tofu, soybean sprouts, scallions and coconut milk. Cut each tofu puff in half diagonally and make a pocket inside with fingers. Fill each puff with about 1$\frac{1}{2}$ teaspoons fish mixture. Brush outside of each puff, including filling, with ketjap manis mixture. Place filled puffs on a prepared baking sheet and bake until lightly browned and crisp, 8–10 minutes.

Tips
• If using homemade tofu puffs, scoop inside out and add it to filling.

• Adding soy sauce to ketjap manis lessens the sweetness of ketjap manis and thins the mixture for easier spreading.

• Substitute red curry paste if Massaman curry paste is unavailable.

Samosas

Makes 12

2¹/₃ cups (12 oz/375 g) all-purpose (plain) flour
salt to taste
3 tablespoons melted butter
about ³/₄ cup (6 fl oz/180 ml) warm water
1 lb (500 g) desiree or pontiac potatoes (about
    3–4 medium), boiled whole and cooled
4 teaspoons vegetable oil
1¹/₂ teaspoons cumin seeds
1 teaspoon finely chopped fresh ginger
¹/₂ teaspoon chili powder
1 small fresh green chili, finely chopped
¹/₄ bunch fresh cilantro (fresh coriander), leaves and
    stems chopped
1 teaspoon chat masala (see page 231)
juice of 1 lemon
salt to taste
vegetable oil, for deep-frying

To make pastry: Sift flour and salt into a bowl. Stir in melted butter. Add enough warm water, cutting into flour mixture with a round-bladed knife, to form a firm dough. Knead dough lightly in bowl until smooth. Wrap in plastic wrap and set aside for 20 minutes.

To make filling: Peel potatoes and mash coarsely in a bowl. In a saucepan over medium heat, heat oil and briefly toast cumin seeds until fragrant. Stir in ginger and then add potatoes, chili powder and chili. Cook, stirring gently, for 3 minutes. Add cilantro, chat masala, lemon juice and salt, and mix well. Remove from heat and let cool.

Divide pastry dough evenly into six portions. Shape each portion into an oval and roll out on a lightly floured work surface until oval is 9 inches (23 cm) long and 5¹/₂ inches (14 cm) wide. Cut each oval in half crosswise. Place one half-oval on your hand with straight edge in line with your forefinger as shown. Wet a finger and run along straight edge to moisten. Place fingers of your other hand in centre of the half-oval, folding in sides so edges overlap to form a cone. Press overlapped edges to seal. Hold cone with open end uppermost.

Spoon one-twelfth of potato mixture into cone and use a wet finger to moisten edge of opening. Pinch edges of opening together to seal and enclose filling. Place samosa on a lightly floured baking sheet.

Repeat with remaining dough and potato filling.

Fill a karhai or wok with vegetable oil to a depth of 5 inches (12.5 cm). Heat oil over medium–high heat to 375°F (190°C) on a deep-frying thermometer. Carefully place four samosas in hot oil and cook, turning often, until crisp and dark golden brown, 3–4 minutes. Use a slotted spoon to remove samosas to paper towels to drain. Serve immediately.

Shrimp fries

Makes 8

8 oz (250 g) jumbo shrimp (green king prawns),
  shelled, deveined and finely chopped

1/2 onion, finely chopped

3 cloves garlic, finely chopped

2 teaspoons peeled and grated fresh ginger

2 tablespoons chopped fresh cilantro (fresh
  coriander)

1 fresh red Thai or Anaheim chili, seeded and finely
  chopped

1/2 teaspoon ground cumin

1/2 teaspoon Garam Masala (see page 223)

2 tablespoons besan flour

2 tablespoons all-purpose (plain) flour

2 cups (16 fl oz/500 ml) vegetable oil, for deep-frying

1 lime, cut into 8 wedges, for serving

In a medium bowl, combine shrimp, onion, garlic, ginger, cilantro, chili, cumin and garam masala. Stir until well combined. Divide into 8 portions and shape into balls. Roll in combined flours.

In a Dutch oven, wok or deep fryer, heat oil to 375°F (190°C), or until a small bread cube dropped in the oil sizzles and turns golden in 1 minute. Add shrimp balls in batches and cook until golden; 2–3 minutes, or until golden. Using a slotted spoon, transfer to paper towels to drain. Serve immediately, with lime wedges.

Tip

Shrimp fries are a great hors d'oeuvre, snack or accompaniment to curry.

Spicy dhal

Serves 4

1 cup (7 oz/220 g) red lentils
2 teaspoons peeled and grated fresh ginger
3 cloves garlic, finely chopped
1 fresh red bird's eye or Thai chili, seeded and
    chopped
1 stalk celery, chopped
2 tablespoons chopped fresh cilantro (fresh coriander)
1 tablespoon fresh lemon juice
5 cups (40 fl oz/1.25 L) water
2 teaspoons tamarind paste
4 scallions (shallots/spring onions), chopped
1 medium carrot, chopped
½ teaspoon garam masala (see page 223)
¼ teaspoon ground turmeric
¼ teaspoon ground coriander
1 teaspoon cumin seeds

Rinse and pick over lentils. In a medium saucepan, combine lentils, ginger, garlic, chili, celery, cilantro, lemon juice, water, tamarind paste, scallions, and carrot. Stir, cover and bring to a boil over high heat. Reduce heat to low and simmer until lentils are tender; 30–40 minutes.

In a blender or food processor, puree lentil mixture in batches until smooth. Return to saucepan.

In a small skillet, combine remaining ingredients and stir over medium heat until fragrant; about 1–2 minutes. Add spice mixture to lentil mixture and stir to blend. Cook over low heat, stirring constantly, until thickened; about 5 minutes. Serve warm or at room temperature, with curries and/or fried pappadams.

Spicy tahini tofu with sesame crackers

Serves 6–8

1 tablespoon superfine (caster) sugar

$^2/_3$ cup (2 oz/60 g) white sesame seeds

2 teaspoons cracked pepper

2 tablespoons tahini (sesame paste)

$^1/_2$ cup (2$^1/_2$ oz/75 g) all-purpose (plain) flour

$^1/_4$ cup (1 oz/30 g) soy flour

2 egg whites, lightly beaten

$^1/_4$ cup (2 fl oz/60 ml) Japanese soy sauce

$^2/_3$ cup (5$^1/_2$ oz/165 g) canned soybeans, drained

5 oz (150 g) soft or silken tofu, drained

$^1/_3$ cup (3 fl oz/90 ml) lemon juice

$^1/_4$ cup (2 oz/60 g) tahini (sesame paste)

2 teaspoons white (shiro) miso

salt and cracked pepper to taste

2 garlic cloves, finely chopped

2 tablespoons finely chopped fresh parsley

1 tablespoon chopped chives

$^1/_4$ teaspoon cayenne pepper or finely chopped,
   seeded chili

To make sesame crackers: Preheat oven to 350°F (180°C/Gas 4). Line a baking sheet, about 12 x 9 inches (30 x 23 cm), with parchment (baking) paper.

In a large bowl, combine sugar, sesame seeds, pepper, tahini, flour, soy flour, egg whites and soy sauce and stir well. Spread mixture thinly onto baking sheet and bake until crisp, 10–15 minutes. Cut into pieces while warm or let cool on tray and break into pieces.

In a food processor, puree soybeans until fairly smooth. Add tofu, lemon juice, tahini, miso, salt, pepper and garlic and process until smooth. Stir in parsley, chives and cayenne. Serve with sesame crackers and vegetable sticks.

Tip

Serve tahini tofu as a sauce with grilled fish or steak.

Spicy tomato salsa and avocado cream in toasted cups

Makes 24

24 slices soy and linseed bread, crusts removed

vegetable oil cooking spray

2 ripe tomatoes, seeded and finely diced

$\frac{1}{3}$ cup (1$\frac{1}{2}$ oz/50 g) finely diced green bell pepper (capsicum)

1 small red (Spanish) onion, finely chopped

1 teaspoon olive oil

1 teaspoon vinegar

$\frac{1}{2}$ teaspoon finely chopped green chili pepper (optional)

salt and cracked pepper to taste

avocado cream (see page 229)

tomato salsa (see page 229)

cilantro (fresh coriander) leaves or mustard cress for garnish

Preheat oven to 400°F (200°C).

Flatten each bread slice with a rolling pin. Cut bread into 3-inch (8-cm) rounds using a cookie (pastry) cutter. Lightly spray both sides of bread slices with cooking spray and press them into muffin cups. Bake until lightly browned and crisp, about 10 minutes. Remove from oven and let cool.

In a bowl, combine tomatoes, bell pepper, onion, oil, vinegar, chili, salt and pepper. Fill each cup with 2 teaspoons avocado cream and 1 teaspoon salsa. Garnish with cilantro and serve immediately as cups will become soft if left standing.

Tip

Bread cases can be made a few days ahead and kept in an airtight container.

Steamed seafood dumplings

Makes 18

8 oz (250 g) firm white-fleshed fish fillets

8 oz (250 g) jumbo shrimp (green king prawns),
peeled and deveined

3 teaspoons peeled and grated fresh ginger

1/2 small red chili, seeded and chopped

3 tablespoons chopped fresh cilantro (fresh coriander)

4 scallions (shallots/spring onions), chopped

1 teaspoon Asian sesame oil

1 teaspoon rice wine

1 teaspoon soy sauce

1/2 teaspoon salt

1 teaspoon sugar

6 canned water chestnuts, drained and finely chopped

18 round wonton wrappers

1/3 cup (3 fl oz/90 ml) soy sauce, for dipping

In a food processor, combine fish fillets and shrimp and process until a thick paste forms, about 30 seconds. Add ginger, chili, cilantro, scallions, sesame oil, rice wine, soy sauce, salt and sugar. Process until well combined, about 10 seconds. Transfer to a bowl and mix in water chestnuts.

Place wonton wrappers on a work surface and keep covered with a damp kitchen towel to prevent drying. Working with one wrapper at a time, lay it on work surface and place 3 teaspoons filling in middle. Gather edges around filling to form a basket. Gently squeeze center of dumpling so that filling is exposed at top. Gently tap bottom of dumpling on work surface to flatten. Set aside, covered with plastic wrap, and repeat with remaining wrappers and filling.

Line a medium-sized bamboo steamer with parchment (baking) paper.

Half fill a medium-sized wok with water (steamer should not touch water) and bring to a boil. Arrange filled wontons in steamer. Cover steamer, place over boiling water and cook for 12 minutes, adding more water to wok when necessary. Lift steamer from wok and carefully remove dumplings. Serve warm with soy sauce for dipping.

Tip

Bird's eye and serrano chilies are recommended for this recipe.

Thai curry fish cakes

Makes 16

1 lb (500 g) redfish or white sea bass fillets, coarsely
chopped

1 tablespoon red curry paste (see page 227)

2 teaspoons fish sauce

2 cloves garlic, coarsely chopped

1 egg yolk

2 teaspoons packed brown sugar

2 scallions (shallots/spring onions), sliced

1 stalk lemongrass, white part only, finely sliced

2 tablespoons chopped fresh cilantro (fresh
coriander)

4 fresh kaffir lime leaves, finely shredded

2 oz (60 g) green beans, trimmed and very thinly
sliced

1 cup (8 fl oz/250 ml) vegetable oil

½ cup (4 fl oz/125 ml) Thai sweet chili sauce

In a food processor, combine fish, curry paste, fish
sauce, garlic, egg and brown sugar. Process to a thick
paste. Transfer to a medium bowl. Add scallions,
lemongrass, cilantro, lime leaves and green beans. Mix
until well combined. Shape into 16 patties. Place on a
plate, cover and refrigerate for 30 minutes.

In a large, heavy skillet, heat oil until surface shimmers
and fry fish cakes in batches until golden, about
1 minute on each side. Using a slotted spoon, transfer
to paper towels to drain. Serve immediately, with Thai
sweet chili sauce.

Tip

As an alternative, make 32 smaller balls and serve with
toothpicks as hors d'oeuvres.

Vegetable spring rolls

Makes 12

1 tablespoon vegetable oil

2 teaspoons Asian sesame oil

1 teaspoon cumin seeds

1 clove garlic, finely chopped

1 tablespoon peeled and grated fresh ginger

2 green Thai or Anaheim chilies, seeded and finely
  chopped

1 teaspoon ground turmeric

1 teaspoon chili powder

1 lb (500 g) potatoes, peeled, boiled and cut into
  1/4-inch (6-mm) cubes

1/2 cup (2 1/2 oz/75 g) fresh or frozen peas

1/2 teaspoon sea salt

1 tablespoon chopped fresh cilantro (fresh coriander)

1 tablespoon chopped fresh mint

12 frozen spring roll wrappers, about 8 inches (20 cm),
  thawed

1 egg white, lightly beaten

3 cups (24 fl oz/750 ml) vegetable oil, for deep-frying

Thai sweet chili sauce and/or soy sauce, for dipping

In a wok or large skillet, heat oils over medium heat. Add
cumin seeds, garlic, ginger, green chilies, turmeric and
chili powder. Fry for 1 minute. Stir in potatoes, peas, and
salt and fry for 1 minute. Remove from heat and let cool
completely. Stir in cilantro and mint.

Place 1 wrapper on a work surface. Place 1 heaped
tablespoon filling in center of wrapper. Fold over sides
and then roll up diagonally. Seal loose edge with egg
white. Repeat with remaining wrappers and filling.

In a wok or deep fryer, heat oil to 375°F (190°C) or until
a small bread cube dropped in the oil sizzles and turns
golden in 1 minute. Add spring rolls in batches and fry
until golden, about 2 minutes. Using a slotted spoon,
transfer to paper towels to drain. Serve immediately
with Thai sweet chili sauce and/or soy sauce.

laksas and soups

Asian fishball soup

Serves 4–6

8 oz (250 g) white-fleshed or oily fish fillets, skinned and ground (minced)

2 teaspoons red curry paste (see page 227)

1 tablespoon chopped fresh cilantro (coriander)

¼ teaspoon salt

1 tablespoon vegetable oil

1 tablespoon chopped lemongrass

1 red chili, seeded and chopped

1 clove garlic, chopped

4 cups (32 fl oz/1 L) fish stock (see page 222)

2 tablespoons fish sauce

1 tablespoon lemon juice

1 cup (4 oz/125 g) sliced oyster mushrooms

3 oz (90 g) soft Asian noodles

½ cup (2 oz/60 g) mung bean sprouts

2 tablespoons chopped fresh mint

In a bowl, combine fish, curry paste, cilantro and salt and mix well. Shape teaspoons of mixture into small balls with wet hands. Set aside.

In a large saucepan over medium heat, heat oil. Add lemongrass, chili and garlic and cook until fragrant, about 1 minute. Pour in stock, fish sauce and lemon juice and bring to boil. Add mushrooms, noodles, and sprouts and simmer for 2 minutes. Add fishballs and mint and simmer until fishballs are tender, a further 2 to 3 minutes.

Serve piping hot.

Beef soup with coconut milk and Thai herbs

Serves 4

2 cloves garlic

2 tablespoons peeled and finely chopped fresh ginger

3 shallots (French shallots), peeled

1 teaspoon galangal powder

½ teaspoon sea salt

½ teaspoon white peppercorns

4 fresh cilantro (fresh coriander) roots

1 small red chili

3 tablespoons light olive oil

12 oz (375 g) round or rump steak, cut into 1-inch (2.5-cm) cubes

5 cups (40 fl oz/1.25 L) coconut milk

3 cups (24 fl oz/750 ml) pho beef stock (see page 218)

2–3 tablespoons lemon juice

2 stalks lemongrass, bottom 4 inches (10 cm) only, cut into 2-inch (5-cm) pieces

3 fresh or 6 dried kaffir lime leaves

2 teaspoons palm sugar or dark brown sugar

1 tablespoon fish sauce

6½ oz (200 g) baby English spinach leaves

In a food processor, combine garlic, ginger, shallots, galangal, salt, peppercorns, cilantro, chili and 2 tablespoons oil. Process to a smooth paste, 1–2 minutes.

In a large saucepan over medium heat, heat remaining oil. Add paste and cook, stirring, until fragrant, 3–4 minutes. Add meat and cook for 3–4 minutes, turning to coat meat and brown it slightly. Add coconut milk, stock and lemon juice and bring mixture to a steady simmer. Add lemongrass, kaffir lime leaves, palm sugar and fish sauce and simmer until meat is tender, about 30 minutes. Remove lemongrass and lime leaves. Season to taste with fish sauce if soup is not salty enough and lemon juice if it is not tangy enough.

Stir in spinach leaves and let soup stand until leaves are wilted, about 1 minute. Serve immediately.

Bok choy and potato soup

Serves 4

¼ cup (2 oz/60 g) butter

2 red (Spanish) onions, chopped

1 clove garlic, chopped

1-inch (2.5-cm) piece fresh ginger, peeled and
  chopped

6 cups (48 fl oz/1.5 L) chicken stock (see page 218) or
  vegetable stock (see 222)

20 oz (625 g) potatoes, peeled and chopped

8 oz (250 g) bok choy, tough stems discarded, leaves
  sliced

1 bunch spinach, stems discarded, leaves sliced

salt and pepper

2 tablespoons soy sauce

14 oz (440 g) udon noodles

1 cup (4 oz/125 g) snow pea (mange-tout) sprouts, for
  garnish

In a large saucepan over medium heat, melt butter. Add
onions, garlic and ginger and cook until onions and garlic
are soft, about 2 minutes. Add stock and bring to a boil.
Add potatoes, reduce heat to simmer, cover and cook
until tender, about 10 minutes.

Add bok choy and spinach. Season with salt and pepper.
Stir in soy sauce and noodles. Cook until noodles are
done, about 5 minutes. Ladle into bowls and garnish with
snow pea sprouts.

Carrot soup with Asian greens and coconut

Serves 4

2 lb (1 kg) carrots, peeled and finely diced

1 large yellow (brown) onion, chopped

2 cloves garlic, chopped

6 cups (48 fl oz/1.5 L) chicken stock (see page 218)
   or vegetable stock (see 222)

6½ oz (200 g) Asian greens such as bok choy or
   choy sum, coarsely sliced

juice of 1 lime

1 tablespoon chopped fresh Thai basil leaves

4 tablespoons thick coconut cream, for serving

¼ cup (1 oz/30 g) unsweetened dried (desiccated)
   shredded coconut, toasted, for garnish

In a large saucepan, combine carrots, onion, garlic and stock. Bring to a boil. Cover and cook until carrots are soft, about 8 minutes. Working in batches, puree soup in a food processor. Return to saucepan and reheat over medium heat, about 5 minutes.

Add greens, lime juice and basil and cook for 2 minutes. Ladle into bowls and top each serving with 1 tablespoon coconut cream. Sprinkle with shredded coconut.

Chicken in coconut milk soup

Serves 4–6

2 cups (16 fl oz/500 ml) coconut cream

1 cup (8 fl oz/125 ml) coconut milk

2 stalks lemongrass, white part only, peeled and cut into 1-inch (2.5-cm) pieces

1/2-inch (12-mm) piece galangal, thinly sliced

2 tablespoons coarsely chopped shallots (French shallots), preferably pink

10–15 small fresh chilies, halved lengthwise

1 cup (4 oz/125 g) canned or 2 cups (8 oz/250 g) fresh straw mushrooms, rinsed, drained and halved

12 oz (375 g) boneless, skinless chicken breasts, thinly sliced

2–3 tablespoons fish sauce to taste

3 fresh kaffir lime leaves, stemmed

1/2 cup (1/2 oz/15 g) coarsely chopped fresh cilantro (fresh coriander)

2 tablespoons fresh lime juice

2 scallions (shallots/spring onions), chopped

In a wok or large saucepan over high heat, combine coconut cream, coconut milk, lemongrass, galangal, shallots, chilies and mushrooms. Bring to a boil, reduce heat and simmer for 3–5 minutes. Add chicken, stirring well. Add fish sauce and lime leaves. Return to a boil. Add half the cilantro and turn off heat.

Stir in lime juice. Transfer to bowls for serving, garnish with scallions and remaining cilantro and serve.

Tips

• For a less rich soup, replace the coconut cream with an equal quantity of coconut milk. For a less spicy broth, keep the chilies whole.

• This is one of Thailand's best-known soups, with a creamy consistency and a lovely lemony flavor. The fibrous ingredients in this dish—kaffir lime leaf, galangal and lemongrass—are not eaten. Just push them aside.

Chili corn soup

Serves 4

3 tablespoons light olive oil
2 red chilies
1 medium yellow (brown) onion
2 cloves garlic, peeled
1 teaspoon dried shrimp paste, optional
2 teaspoons finely grated lime zest (rind)
1 tablespoon chopped fresh ginger or fresh galangal
   or 2 teaspoons galangal powder
1 tablespoon coriander seeds
1 teaspoon cumin seeds
1/2 teaspoon fennel seeds
1/2 teaspoon ground cardamom
8 cups (64 fl oz/2 L) chicken stock (see page 218) or
   vegetable stock (see 222)
4 cups (24 oz/750 g) fresh or frozen corn kernels
2 teaspoons fish sauce
1 tablespoon lime juice
1 roasted red bell pepper (capsicum), peeled and
   seeded
1 teaspoon chili paste or sambal oelek (see page 228)

In a food processor, combine 2 tablespoons oil, chilies, onion, garlic, shrimp paste, lime zest, ginger and spices. Process to a smooth paste, 2–3 minutes.

In a large saucepan over medium heat, heat remaining oil and add paste. Cook, stirring, until fragrant, 3–4 minutes. Add stock, increase heat to medium–high and bring liquid to a steady simmer. Add corn, fish sauce and lime juice and simmer until corn is tender, about 5 minutes.

Let soup cool slightly. Working in batches if necessary, ladle into a food processor and process until smooth, 2–3 minutes. Return to saucepan and reheat before serving.

In a food processor, process bell pepper and chili paste until smooth, about 2 minutes.

Ladle soup into individual bowls and garnish with a little chili paste.

Classic beef pho

Serves 4

12 oz (375 g) lean beef fillet
10 oz (300 g) fresh thick rice noodles
6 oz (180 g) small green beans, trimmed
6 oz (180 g) snow peas (mange-tout), trimmed
1 small bunch fresh cilantro (fresh coriander),
   separated into sprigs
1 cup (1 oz/30 g) small fresh basil leaves
5 oz (150 g) bean sprouts, trimmed
8 cups (64 fl oz/2 L) pho beef stock (see page 218)
1 lime, quartered
chili sauce or sambal oelek, to taste (see page 228)
2 tablespoons fish sauce to taste (optional)

Wrap beef fillet in plastic wrap and freeze until it is firm and beginning to freeze completely, about 1 hour. Remove from freezer and slice as thinly as possible. Set aside at room temperature and allow to defrost completely.

Bring a large pot of water to a boil and add rice noodles. Cook until noodles are tender, 3–4 minutes. Drain noodles and place in a colander.

Bring a small saucepan with 1 inch (2.5 cm) water to a boil. Add green beans and snow peas and cook for 1 minute. Drain immediately and place in a bowl with cilantro, basil and bean sprouts. Set aside.

In a saucepan, heat stock until boiling. Rinse noodles under very hot water quickly, using a fork to separate them. Divide among 4 bowls. Pour stock over noodles and top with beef slices.

Allow to stand for 1–2 minutes. Top with herbs and vegetables. Add a squeeze of lime, and chili sauce and fish sauce to taste.

Coconut shrimp soup

Serves 4

1 lb (500 g) jumbo shrimp (green king prawns)

1 lemongrass stalk, chopped, or 2 teaspoons grated
lemon zest (rind)

1 carrot, peeled and sliced

1 celery stalk, sliced

1 onion, sliced

2 plum (Roma) tomatoes, chopped

1 bunch fresh cilantro (fresh coriander)

6 cups (48 fl oz/1.5 L) water

2 cups (16 fl oz/500 ml) coconut milk

1½ tablespoons red curry paste (see page 227)

1 teaspoon palm sugar or brown sugar

2 teaspoons fish sauce

8 oz (250 g) hokkien noodles

juice of 2 limes

Peel and devein shrimp; reserve heads and shells. Cover shrimp and set aside.

In a large saucepan, combine shrimp heads and shells. Add lemongrass or zest, carrot, celery, onion and tomatoes. Remove cilantro leaves from stems. Chop stems and add to saucepan; chop and reserve leaves. Pour in water. Bring to boil, reduce heat to low, cover and simmer gently, stirring occasionally, for 20 minutes. Strain through fine-mesh sieve. Measure 5 cups (40 fl oz/1.25 L) stock.

Return measured stock to saucepan. Stir in coconut milk, curry paste, sugar, fish sauce, noodles, lime juice, cilantro leaves and shrimp. Bring to boil, reduce heat to low, cover and simmer, stirring occasionally, until shrimp change color, 6–7 minutes.

Ladle into individual bowls and serve.

Combination soup

Serves 4

3 dried shiitake mushrooms

3½ oz (105 g) thin, dried rice noodles

1 tablespoon light olive oil

¼ cup (⅓ oz/10 g) finely chopped fresh cilantro (fresh coriander)

½ teaspoon ground white pepper

2 cloves garlic, finely chopped

3 oz (90 g) pork fillet, trimmed of fat and sinew, thinly sliced

6 oz (180 g) skinless, boneless chicken breast, thinly sliced

8 cups (64 fl oz/2 L) chicken stock (see page 218)

1 tablespoon fish sauce

6 oz (180 g) medium shrimp (prawns), peeled and deveined

¼ cup (¾ oz/25 g) chopped scallions (shallots/spring onions)

1 egg, lightly beaten

1 small cucumber, sliced, for garnish

Soak dried mushrooms in a small bowl of hot water for 30 minutes. Remove from water, cut off and discard stems and slice caps. Set aside.

Place noodles in a bowl, pour boiling water over and allow to stand until soft, 7–8 minutes. Drain and set aside.

In a large saucepan over medium heat, heat oil. Add cilantro, white pepper, garlic, pork, chicken and mushrooms and cook, stirring, for 3 minutes. Add stock and fish sauce and bring liquid to a steady simmer. Simmer for 15 minutes. Stir in shrimp and scallions and cook until shrimp are cooked through, 2–3 minutes. Increase heat to high and bring liquid to a boil. As soon as it boils, briskly stir in egg. Liquid must be boiling or egg will not set.

Rinse noodles under very hot water, using a fork to separate them, then spoon into individual bowls. Ladle soup over noodles and serve topped with cucumber.

Curried parsnip soup with parsnip chips

Serves 6

¼ cup (2 fl oz/60 ml) vegetable oil

1 large onion, chopped

2 cloves garlic, crushed

1 teaspoon ground turmeric

½ teaspoon ground cumin

½ teaspoon ground ginger

½ small chili, seeded and sliced

1¼ lb (625 g) parsnips, peeled and chopped

2 cooking apples, peeled, cored and chopped

4 cups (32 fl oz/1 L) vegetable stock (see page 222)

sea salt and freshly ground black pepper to taste

1 cup (8 fl oz/250 ml) cream

For parsnip chips

4 parsnips, peeled

3 cups (24 fl oz/750 ml) vegetable oil, for deep-frying

In a large saucepan over medium heat, warm oil. Add onion and garlic and cook until onion softens, about 2 minutes. Stir in turmeric, cumin, ginger and chili, and cook for 3 minutes, stirring occasionally. Add parsnips and apples and stir well. Cover and cook for 5 minutes, stirring occasionally. Stir in stock and season with salt and pepper. Bring mixture to a boil over high heat, then reduce heat, cover and simmer until parsnips are soft, 30–40 minutes.

To make parsnip chips: Using a vegetable peeler, thinly slice each parsnip lengthwise. In a large, deep, heavy-bottomed saucepan or deep-fat fryer, heat oil until it reaches 375°F (190°C) on a deep-frying thermometer or until a small cube of bread dropped into oil sizzles and turns golden. Working in handfuls, add parsnip slices to hot oil and deep-fry until golden, about 1 minute. Using a slotted spoon, remove chips from oil and drain on paper towels.

Remove soup from heat and transfer to a large bowl. Working in batches, ladle into a food processor and process until smooth, about 20 seconds. Return soup to saucepan and heat through over medium heat, about 5 minutes. Stir in cream just before serving. Ladle into serving bowls and top with crisp parsnip chips.

Curry yogurt soup

Serves 2

2 tablespoons vegetable oil

1 green Thai or Anaheim chili, seeded and chopped

4 cloves garlic, finely chopped

1 tablespoon peeled and grated fresh ginger

4 dried red chilies

1 teaspoon cumin seeds

1/2 teaspoon chili powder

1/2 teaspoon ground turmeric

8 fresh curry leaves

2 cups (16 oz/500 g) plain (natural) yogurt

sea salt to taste

1/2 cup (4 fl oz/125 ml) coconut milk

1/4 fresh red Thai or Anaheim chili, seeded and cut
  into very fine 2-inch (5-cm) lengths

In a medium saucepan, heat 1 tablespoon oil over medium heat and fry chili, garlic, ginger, dried chilies, cumin seeds, chili powder, turmeric, and 4 of the curry leaves until fragrant, 2–3 minutes. Reduce heat to low and stir in yogurt and salt. Cook for 5 minutes, stirring (do not boil). Stir in coconut milk and cook for 1 minute, stirring constantly. Remove and discard dried chilies. Spoon into serving bowls.

In a small skillet, heat remaining 1 tablespoon oil and fry remaining 4 curry leaves and shredded fresh red chili until the chili curls, about 30 seconds. Using a slotted spoon, transfer to paper towels to drain. Garnish each soup bowl with curry and chili leaf mixture.

Hot and sour chicken soup

Serves 4

For tom yum stock

2 tablespoons vegetable oil

1 teaspoon chili powder

2 tablespoons dried shrimp

1 stalk lemongrass, bottom 3 inches (7.5 cm) only, chopped

1 clove garlic, chopped

4 black peppercorns

1 teaspoon galangal powder or 1 tablespoon chopped fresh galangal

1 red chili

1 green chili

3 fresh or 6 dried kaffir lime leaves

2 tablespoons fish sauce

2 tablespoons lime juice

1/2 teaspoon shrimp paste

2 teaspoons finely grated lime zest (rind)

8 cups (64 fl oz/2 L) chicken stock (see page 218)

For soup

2 teaspoons peanut oil

1 red (Spanish) onion, sliced

1 medium carrot, julienned

skinless, boneless chicken breasts, 8 oz (250 g) each, sliced

3 oz (90 g) small button mushrooms, sliced (optional)

tom yum stock

4 fresh or 8 dried kaffir lime leaves

lime juice and fish sauce to taste

4 fresh basil sprigs, for garnish

To make tom yum stock: In a large saucepan over medium heat, heat vegetable oil until hot, about 1 minute. Add chili powder and stir until oil becomes red, 3–4 minutes. Set aside. Place dried shrimp in a food processor and process until fine, 2–3 minutes. Add remaining ingredients, except chicken stock, and process to a smooth paste, about 3 minutes. Return chili oil to heat and add paste. Cook, stirring, until oil comes to surface, 3–4 minutes. Add chicken stock and bring mixture to a steady simmer. Simmer for 15 minutes. Strain mixture through a fine sieve and set aside. Discard solids.

To make soup: In a large saucepan over medium heat, heat peanut oil until hot, about 1 minute. Add onion and carrot. Cook, stirring, until just soft, 4–5 minutes. Add chicken, mushrooms and tom yum stock and bring to a steady simmer. Add lime leaves and simmer until chicken is cooked through, about 10 minutes. Season to taste with lime juice and fish sauce, 1 teaspoon at a time. Remove lime leaves. Ladle into individual bowls and serve each bowl garnished with a basil sprig.

Hot and sour shrimp soup

Serves 4

1 lb (500 g) green shrimp (prawns), peeled, heads and
shells reserved

8 cups (64 fl oz/2 L) water

1 medium white onion, chopped

2 stalks lemongrass, bottom 3 inches (7.5 cm) only,
cut into 1-inch (2.5-cm) lengths

4 fresh or 8 dried kaffir lime leaves

1 tablespoon fish sauce

3 tablespoons lime juice

1 long red chili, thinly sliced

1 small red (Spanish) onion, thinly sliced

1 large carrot, peeled and sliced into rounds or flowers
(see Tip below)

8 large sprigs fresh cilantro (fresh coriander), for
garnish

In a large saucepan, combine shrimp heads and shells,
water, white onion, half the lemongrass and half the kaffir
lime leaves. Bring mixture to a boil over high heat then
reduce heat to medium and simmer for 25 minutes. Strain
mixture through a fine sieve and discard solids.

Pour stock into a large saucepan and add remaining
lemongrass and kaffir lime leaves, fish sauce, lime juice,
chili, red onion and carrot. Simmer over medium heat until
carrots are tender, about 10 minutes. Add shrimp and
simmer until cooked through, 3–4 minutes. Adjust
seasonings by adding more fish sauce if soup is not salty
enough or more lime juice if it is not tangy enough.

Remove kaffir lime leaves and ladle soup into individual
bowls. Serve immediately, topped with cilantro sprigs.

Tip

To make carrot flowers: Cut carrots into slices 1/8 inch
(3 mm) thick. Make flowers using small, flower-shaped
cookie (pastry) cutter.

Marinated beef laksa

Serves 4

10 oz (300 g) lean beef fillet

3 tablespoons lime juice

3 tablespoons light olive oil

1 teaspoon chili oil

1 small red chili, chopped

2 scallions (shallots/spring onions), white part only, finely chopped

1 clove garlic, minced

2 tablespoons finely chopped fresh cilantro (coriander)

¼ cup (2 oz/60 g) laksa paste (see Penang laksa, page 63)

4 cups (32 fl oz/1 L) beef or vegetable stock (see page 222)

4 cups (32 fl oz/1 L) coconut milk

2 teaspoons fish sauce

2 cups (4 oz/125 g) baby spinach leaves

4 oz (125 g) mixed fresh mushrooms (enoki, cremini, shiitake and button), sliced if large, for garnish

4 oz (125 g) deep-fried tofu (about 4 puffs), sliced, for garnish

4 large sprigs fresh cilantro (fresh coriander), for garnish

¼ cup (2 oz/60 g) crispy fried onions or shallots (French shallots), for garnish (see seafood laksa, page 66)

Wrap beef fillet in plastic wrap and freeze until partially frozen, about 1 hour. Remove from freezer and slice into very thin strips. Place in a ceramic or glass bowl and add 1 tablespoon lime juice, 1 tablespoon olive oil, chili oil, chili, scallions, garlic and cilantro. Mix gently to combine marinade ingredients. Cover and refrigerate for 1 hour.

In a large saucepan over medium–high heat, heat remaining oil until hot, about 1 minute. Add laksa paste and cook, stirring, until very fragrant, about 5 minutes. Add remaining lime juice, stock, coconut milk and fish sauce, reduce heat to medium and bring mixture to a steady simmer. Simmer for 15 minutes. Stir in spinach and simmer until leaves have wilted, about 1 minute.

Remove beef from refrigerator. Ladle soup into individual bowls and add beef and marinade. Top with garnishes, finishing with crispy fried onions. The beef and mushrooms will cook in the stock. Serve immediately.

Mussels in spice coconut milk broth

Serves 4

1 large yellow (brown) onion, sliced

3 cloves garlic

1 teaspoon ground coriander

1/4 teaspoon turmeric

2 small red chilies

1 stalk lemongrass, bottom 3 inches (7.5 cm) only,
  chopped

2 tablespoons lemon juice

1 tablespoon light olive oil

2 cups (16 fl oz/500 ml) fish stock (see page 222)

2 cups (16 fl oz/500 ml) coconut milk

2 teaspoons fish sauce

4 lb (2 kg) mussels in their shells, scrubbed

2-inch (5-cm) piece fresh ginger, very finely sliced
  lengthwise and julienned

1/2 cup (1/2 oz/15 g) fresh cilantro (fresh coriander) leaves

In a food processor, combine onion, garlic, coriander, turmeric, chilies, lemongrass and lemon juice. Process mixture to a fine paste, 2–3 minutes.

In a very large saucepan, with a lid, heat oil over medium heat and add paste. Cook, stirring, until fragrant, about 5 minutes. Add fish stock, coconut milk and fish sauce, increase heat to high and bring liquid to a boil. Add mussels, then cover saucepan tightly and cook, shaking saucepan occasionally, until all mussels have opened, 7–8 minutes. Discard any mussels that did not open. Add ginger and cilantro and stir to combine thoroughly.

Serve immediately in large bowls.

1 teaspoon ground coriander

¼ teaspoon turmeric

2 cups (16 fl oz/500 ml) coconut milk

4 cups (32 fl oz/1 L) fish stock (see page 222)

8 oz (250 g) deep-fried tofu

4 sprigs fresh mint

4 sprigs fresh basil

1 small red (Spanish) onion, very thinly sliced

1 small cucumber, sliced and julienned

1 red chili sliced (optional)

¼ cup (2 oz/60 g) crispy fried onions or shallots
(French shallots) (see seafood laksa, page 66)

In a glass or ceramic bowl, combine sesame oil, 2 tablespoons fish sauce, 2 tablespoons lime juice, honey, chili, cilantro and mint. Add octopus and squid, then cover and refrigerate. Allow to marinate for 3 hours.

In a large saucepan over medium–high heat, heat peanut oil. Add chopped onion, ginger, garlic, chili paste, ground coriander and turmeric and cook, stirring, until onion is soft and mixture is fragrant, about 5 minutes. Add remaining lime juice, coconut milk, fish stock and remaining fish sauce. Bring liquid to a boil, then reduce heat to medium–low and simmer for 15–20 minutes.

Preheat broiler (grill). Remove squid and octopus from marinade and discard marinade. Broil (grill) squid and octopus until cooked through and tender, 3–4 minutes for squid, 4–5 minutes for octopus.

Add squid and octopus to simmering soup and stir to combine. Ladle into individual bowls and pile high with remaining ingredients, finishing with crispy fried onions.

Octopus and squid laksa

Serves 4

1 tablespoon Asian sesame oil

3 tablespoons fish sauce

5 tablespoons (3 fl oz/80 ml) lime juice

1 tablespoon honey

2 small red chili, finely chopped

¼ cup (¼ oz/7 g) finely chopped fresh cilantro
(fresh coriander)

2 tablespoons finely chopped fresh mint

8 oz (250 g) baby octopus, trimmed of head and beak

8 oz (250 g) small whole squid, cleaned, trimmed
and cut into rings ½ inch (12 mm) thick

1 tablespoon peanut oil

1 medium yellow (brown) onion, chopped

2 tablespoons grated fresh ginger

2 teaspoons crushed garlic

1 tablespoon chili paste or sambal oelek (see
page 228)

Penang laksa

Serves 4

2 tablespoons peanut oil

1 medium yellow (brown) onion, sliced

2 tablespoons laksa paste (see below)

8 cups (64 fl oz/2 L) fish stock (see page 222)

¼ cup (2 fl oz/60 ml) lime or lemon juice

7 oz (220 g) dried rice noodles

1 lb (500 g) firm white-fleshed fish fillets, skin and
  bones removed, cut into 8 pieces

8 oz (250 g) scallops or shrimp (prawns)

4 deep-fried tofu puffs, halved

5 oz (150 g) bean sprouts, trimmed

4 quail eggs, hard-cooked (boiled), peeled and
  halved or 2 hard-cooked (boiled) chicken eggs,
  peeled and quartered)

4 small sprigs fresh mint

4 small sprigs fresh basil

¼ cup crispy fried onions

In a large saucepan over medium heat, heat oil. Add onion and cook until it begins to soften, 3–4 minutes. Add laksa paste and continue to cook, stirring, until onion is soft and paste is fragrant, about 4 minutes. Add fish stock and lime juice, increase heat to medium–high and bring liquid to a steady simmer. Reduce heat to medium–low and simmer for 10 minutes.

Meanwhile, place noodles in a large bowl and add boiling water to cover. Allow to stand until noodles are soft, 3–5 minutes. Drain, rinse noodles in very hot water and set aside.

Add fish to laksa broth and simmer until cooked through, 4–5 minutes. Add scallops and tofu and cook for 1 minute.

Rinse noodles under very hot water, using a fork to keep them separate.

Spoon noodles into individual bowls and ladle soup over top, piling fish and scallops in middle. Top with remaining ingredients, finishing with crispy fried onions. Serve immediately.

For laksa paste

¾ cup (4 oz/125 g) dried shrimp

12 dried red chilies

6–8 scallions (shallots/spring onions), about 6½ oz
  (200 g), coarsely chopped

6 cloves garlic

4-inch (10-cm) piece fresh ginger, peeled and
  coarsely chopped

2 teaspoons dried shrimp paste

2 stalks lemongrass, bottom 3 inches (7.5 cm) only,
  chopped

½ cup (3 oz/90 g) candlenuts or blanched almonds

1 tablespoon ground turmeric

½ cup (4 fl oz/125 ml) light olive oil

In a bowl, combine shrimp and chilies and add enough boiling water to cover. Let stand for 15 minutes. Drain, then place shrimp and chili mixture in a food processor with remaining ingredients. Process mixture to a fine paste, 2–3 minutes. Transfer paste to a bowl or sterilized jar, then cover and refrigerate.

Potato soup with Thai spices

Serves 4

2 tablespoons olive oil

1 yellow (brown) onion, chopped

2 cloves garlic, chopped

20 oz (625 g) potatoes, peeled and coarsely
chopped

2 tablespoons chopped fresh cilantro (fresh coriander)

2 tablespoons chopped fresh flat-leaf (Italian) parsley

4 fresh kaffir lime leaves or 1 teaspoon grated lime
zest (rind)

1 tablespoon peeled and grated fresh ginger

1 small red chili, seeded and chopped

6 cups (48 fl oz/1.5 L) vegetable stock (see
page 222) or water

salt and pepper

1½ cups (12 fl oz/375 ml) coconut milk

4 fresh kaffir lime leaves or 1 teaspoon grated lime
zest (rind), for garnish

In a large saucepan over medium heat, warm oil. Add onion and garlic and cook until onion softens, about 2 minutes. Add potatoes, cilantro, parsley, 4 lime leaves, ginger and chili and cook for 1 minute. Add stock and bring to a boil. Reduce heat to simmer, cover and cook until potatoes are tender, 20–25 minutes. Remove lime leaves and discard.

Break up some of the potatoes with a potato masher, keeping texture of soup chunky. Season with salt and pepper. Add coconut milk and heat through, about 2 minutes. Serve warm, garnishing each portion with a lime leaf.

Tip

Bird's eye and serrano chilies are recommended for this recipe.

Quick-and-easy chicken laksa

Serves 4

1½ tablespoons peanut oil

7 oz (220 g) skinless, boneless chicken thigh meat,
  sliced into strips

2 teaspoons chili paste or sambal oelek (see page 228)

3 cloves garlic, minced, or 2 teaspoons prepared
  crushed garlic

2-inch (5-cm) piece fresh ginger, peeled and finely
  grated, or 2 teaspoons prepared crushed ginger

1 teaspoon ground coriander

½ teaspoon turmeric

1 teaspoon dark brown sugar

grated zest (rind) of 1 lemon (about 2 teaspoons)

¼ cup (2 fl oz/60 ml) lemon juice

1 tablespoon fish sauce

6 cups (48 fl oz/1.5 L) chicken stock (see page 218)

2 cups (16 fl oz/500 ml) coconut milk

8 oz (250 g) fresh egg noodles

8 oz (250 g) deep-fried tofu

5 oz (150 g) bean sprouts, trimmed

1 small cucumber, sliced and quartered

3 scallions (shallots/spring onions), sliced

½ cup (½ oz/15 g) fresh cilantro (fresh coriander) sprigs

lime wedges, for serving (optional)

In a large saucepan over medium–high heat, heat oil. Add
chicken strips and cook, turning frequently, until slightly
brown, about 4 minutes. Add chili paste, garlic, ginger,
coriander, turmeric, brown sugar and lemon zest and cook,
stirring, until spices are aromatic, 3–4 minutes. Add lemon
juice, fish sauce, chicken stock and coconut milk. Increase
heat to high and bring mixture to a steady simmer. Reduce
heat to medium–low and simmer for 15 minutes.

Meanwhile, bring a large saucepan of water to a boil and
add noodles. Cook until noodles are tender, 5–7 minutes,
then drain and rinse noodles under very hot water.

Place noodles in individual bowls and ladle soup over top.
Top with tofu, bean sprouts, cucumber, scallions and
cilantro and serve immediately. Serve with lime wedges.

Ramen and roast duck soup

Serves 4

6½ oz (200 g) ramen noodles

2 cups (16 fl oz/500 ml) chicken stock (see
 page 218)

3 cups (24 fl oz/750 ml) water

5 thin slices fresh ginger

4 small red chilies, seeded, if desired, and
 halved

2 teaspoons lime juice

3 lemongrass stalks, bruised

3 fresh cilantro (fresh coriander) roots, bruised

1 Chinese roasted duck, meat removed and chopped

4 scallions (shallots/spring onions), chopped

½ cup (2 oz/60 g) fresh bean sprouts, rinsed

¼ cup (⅓ oz/10 g) chopped fresh cilantro (fresh
 coriander)

Cook noodles as directed on package or on page 23. Drain and set aside. In a saucepan, combine stock, water, ginger, 4 chili halves and lime juice. Bring to a boil, reduce heat to low, cover and simmer, stirring occasionally, until flavors are blended, about 5 minutes. Add lemongrass and cilantro roots. Simmer, stirring occasionally, for 15 minutes. Strain through fine-mesh sieve. Return stock to saucepan.

Add duck meat, scallions and noodles to stock and simmer until heated through, about 5 minutes.

Ladle into individual bowls. Top each serving with bean sprouts, fresh cilantro and remaining chili halves.

Tip

Chinese roasted duck is available at Asian markets. Be sure to ask for the duck whole, not chopped on the bone.

Seafood laksa

Serves 4

1½ tablespoons light olive oil

½ cup (4 oz/125 g) laksa paste (see Penang laksa, page 63)

2 tablespoons lime or lemon juice

3 cups (24 fl oz/750 ml) coconut milk

3 cups (24 fl oz/750 ml) fish stock (see page 222)

6 oz (180 g) dried rice vermicelli noodles

12 oz (375 g) medium shrimp (prawns), peeled and deveined, tails left intact

16 oz (500 g) salmon fillet, cut into 8 pieces, 1 inch (5 cm) thick

1 medium red (Spanish) onion, thinly sliced

1 medium cucumber, peeled and sliced

7 oz (220 g) bean sprouts, trimmed

5 oz (150 g) mustard cress shoots or snow pea (mange-tout) shoots

1 medium mango, 12 oz (375 g), peeled, pitted and diced

2 tablespoons small mint leaves

¼ cup (2 oz/60 g) crispy fried shallots (French shallots) (see below)

Heat oil in a large saucepan over medium–high heat. Stir in laksa paste and cook, stirring, until fragrant, 4–5 minutes. Add lime juice, coconut milk and stock and stir until thoroughly combined. Reduce heat to medium and simmer for 10 minutes.

Place noodles in a large bowl and add boiling water to cover. Let stand until noodles are soft, 3–4 minutes. Drain noodles, rinse under warm water and set aside. Add shrimp and salmon to soup and simmer until shrimp are cooked through and salmon is just cooked through, 3–4 minutes.

Rinse noodles under very hot water, using a fork to separate them.

Spoon noodles into individual bowls and top with soup and seafood. Top with remaining ingredients, finishing with crispy fried shallots. Serve immediately.

For crispy fried shallots (french shallots)

2 cups (16 fl oz/500 ml) peanut oil

5 or 6 medium shallots (French shallots), about 5 oz (150 g), peeled and very thinly sliced

In a medium saucepan over high heat, heat oil until it reaches 375°F (190°C) on a deep-frying thermometer. Add shallots all at once and fry until golden, about 1½ minutes. Using a slotted spoon, transfer to a plate lined with paper towels.

Spicy crab and rice noodle soup

Serves 6

3 lb (1.5 kg) raw or cooked crab in its shell or 1½ lb (24 oz/750 g) lump crabmeat, picked over for shell

6 cups (48 fl oz/1.5 L) water or, if using precooked crab, fish stock (see page 222)

3 tablespoons vegetable oil

1 cup (4 oz/125 g) thinly sliced pink or brown shallots (French shallots)

¼ cup (2 fl oz/60 ml) Asian chili sauce (see page 230)

12-oz (375-g) packet dried rice noodles

1 bunch spinach (English spinach), stemmed and rinsed well

2 tablespoons fish sauce, plus more for serving

1–2 teaspoons salt to taste

freshly ground pepper to taste

1–2 lemons, quartered

If using raw crabs, scrub them with a scouring brush under cold running water, then plunge them into a deep pot of lightly salted boiling water—about 6 cups (48 fl oz/1.5 L). Cook for 10–15 minutes, depending on size. Remove crabs with a slotted spoon, reserving cooking liquid. Clean crabs by pulling off apron flap from under shell. Pry off top shell and rinse away breathing ducts or lungs. Break or cut body in half, or cut large crabs into smaller pieces. Twist off claws, reserving pincers for garnish. Refrigerate until ready to use.

In a small saucepan, heat oil over medium heat and sauté one-quarter of shallots with the chili sauce until shallots are soft, 3–5 minutes; set aside.

Prepare dried noodles as directed on package or on page 23.

Bring 6 cups reserved cooking liquid from crab (or stock if using precooked crab), to a rapid boil. Add remaining ³⁄₄ cup shallots, spinach, crab and 2 tablespoons fish sauce. Stir to combine and taste, adding salt if necessary. Remove from heat to avoid overcooking crab.

Immediately prior to serving, reheat noodles by plunging them into boiling water for a moment, then drain. Divide among warmed large, deep soup bowls. Ladle hot soup over noodles, sprinkle with pepper and add a dollop of reserved cooked chili sauce to each (this dish is traditionally served very spicy). Serve piping hot, with additional fish sauce to taste and lemon quarters on the side.

Spicy squash and bean soup

Serves 4

2 tablespoons olive oil

3 scallions (shallots/spring onions), finely sliced

12 oz (375 g) carrots, peeled and sliced

5 oz (150 g) rutabaga (swede), peeled and cubed

2 celery stalks, sliced

1 lb (500 g) pumpkin or butternut squash, peeled and cubed

1 small red chili, seeded and sliced

¾ cup (5 oz/150 g) drained, canned cannellini beans

6 cups (48 fl oz/1.5 L) vegetable stock (see page 222)

1 bay leaf

6 sprigs fresh cilantro (fresh coriander), leaves removed and stems tied with kitchen string

1 cup (8 fl oz/250 ml) cream

2 tablespoons chopped fresh Vietnamese mint, for garnish

2 tablespoons chopped fresh cilantro (fresh coriander), for garnish

In large pan over medium heat, warm oil. Add scallions, carrots, rutabaga, celery, squash and chili and cook until vegetables soften slightly, about 6 minutes. Add beans, stock, bay leaf and cilantro leaves and stems. Bring to a boil. Cover, reduce heat to low and cook until vegetables are tender, about 15 minutes. Remove cilantro stems and discard.

Working in batches, puree soup in a food processor or blender. Return to saucepan and heat through, about 3 minutes. Ladle into bowls and swirl ¼ cup (2 fl oz/60 ml) cream into each serving. Combine chopped mint and cilantro. Garnish soup with herbs and serve immediately.

Tip
Bird's eye and serrano chilies are recommended for this recipe.

Sweet potato and roast duck soup

Serves 4

2 medium sweet potatoes

1 tablespoon light olive oil, plus 2 teaspoons

2 large red (Spanish) onions, very thinly sliced

3 cloves garlic, minced

2-inch (5-cm) piece fresh ginger, peeled and grated

8 cups (64 fl oz/2 L) chicken stock (see page 218)

2 small red chilies, thinly sliced

grated zest (rind) of 1 lime

1 Chinese roasted duck, meat removed from bones

1 teaspoon fish sauce

2 tablespoons lime juice

freshly ground black pepper

1/2 cup (1/2 oz/15 g) fresh cilantro (fresh coriander) leaves
   plus 4 sprigs for garnish

1/2 cup (1/2 oz/15 g) small fresh basil leaves

1/2 cup (1/2 oz/15 g) small fresh mint leaves

Preheat oven to 400°F (200°C/Gas 6). Place sweet potatoes on an oven rack and bake until a skewer inserted through thickest part meets with no resistance, 30–40 minutes. Remove sweet potatoes from oven and set aside to cool. When cool enough to handle, remove skins and chop flesh into pieces.

In a large saucepan over medium heat, heat 1 tablespoon oil. Add half the onion slices, half the garlic and half the ginger and cook, stirring, for 3–4 minutes. Add chicken stock and bring liquid to a steady simmer. Simmer for 15 minutes. Reduce heat to medium–low and add chopped sweet potato. Cook for 2–3 minutes, then remove from heat and allow to cool slightly. Place mixture, working in batches, in a food processor and puree until smooth, about 3 minutes. Return pureed mixture to large saucepan and keep hot enough to serve.

In a large frying pan or wok, heat remaining oil. Add remaining onion, chilies, remaining garlic and ginger, lime zest and duck and cook, tossing and stirring, for 1 minute. Remove from heat and add fish sauce, lime juice, black pepper, cilantro, basil and mint. Stir until combined.

Ladle soup into individual bowls, top with the duck mixture and serve immediately.

Three lentil spicy broth

Serves 4–6

$\frac{1}{2}$ cup ($3\frac{1}{2}$ oz/105 g) black lentils, rinsed and drained

$\frac{1}{2}$ cup (2 oz/60 g) dried red kidney beans, rinsed and drained

$\frac{1}{4}$ cup (2 oz/60 g) split chickpeas (garbanzo beans), rinsed and drained

5 cups (40 fl oz/1.25 L) water

$2\frac{1}{2}$-inch (6-cm) cinnamon stick

3 green cardamom pods, cracked

3 whole cloves

$1\frac{1}{2}$ tablespoons finely grated fresh ginger

$1\frac{1}{2}$ tablespoons crushed garlic

2–4 teaspoons chili powder

14 oz (440 g) canned crushed peeled tomatoes

$\frac{2}{3}$ cup (5 oz/150 g) unsalted butter, chopped

salt to taste

4 teaspoons dried fenugreek leaves, crushed

Place lentils, kidney beans, chickpeas and water in a large bowl. Cover and let stand overnight.

The next day, place lentil mixture and liquid in a large, heavy saucepan. Place cinnamon, cardamom and cloves in a square of cheesecloth (muslin), bring up the corners to form a bundle, tie with kitchen twine and add to pan. Bring to a boil. Reduce heat to low and cook, uncovered, until lentils, beans and chickpeas are tender, about $1\frac{1}{2}$ hours. Add extra water if necessary to keep lentil mixture covered.

Remove bundle of spices and discard. Add ginger, garlic, chili powder, tomatoes, butter and salt to pan. Raise heat to medium and cook, stirring often, for 10 minutes. The consistency should be like thick soup. If too thick, add a small amount of water. Taste and adjust seasoning. Stir in fenugreek leaves.

Tip

Steamed basmati rice or paratha bread accompanies this soup perfectly.

Tom yam soup with shrimp

Serves 4–6

12 oz (375 g) jumbo shrimp (green king prawns)

3 cups (24 fl oz/750 ml) chicken stock (see
   page 218) or water

2 stalks lemongrass, white part only, cut into 1-inch
   (2.5-cm) pieces

6 cloves garlic, crushed

3 tablespoons coarsely chopped shallots (French
   shallots), preferably pink

1-inch (2.5-cm) piece fresh galangal, thinly sliced

2 firm tomatoes, cut into 8 wedges

1 cup (4 oz/125 g) canned or 2 cups (8 oz/250 g)
fresh straw mushrooms, rinsed, drained and halved

10 small fresh green chilies, stems removed and
   halved lengthwise

2–3 tablespoons fish sauce to taste

5 kaffir lime leaves, coarsely torn

2 tablespoons fresh lime juice

1/2 cup (1/2 oz/15 g) coarsely chopped fresh cilantro
   (fresh coriander) leaves and stems

Shell and devein shrimp, leaving tails intact and reserving shells and heads.

In a medium saucepan, combine shrimp heads, shells and stock or water, and bring to a boil. Using a skimmer, remove and discard the heads and shells. Bring back to a boil. Add lemongrass, garlic, shallots and galangal to the stock, then tomatoes, mushrooms, chilies, fish sauce to taste and kaffir lime leaves. Simmer gently for 2 minutes then increase heat and return to a boil.

Add shrimp and briskly boil for no more than 1 minute. Remove from heat and stir in lime juice. Transfer to bowls for serving, garnish with fresh cilantro and serve.

Tips

• The fibrous ingredients in this dish—kaffir lime leaf, galangal and lemongrass—are not eaten. Just push them aside when eating the soup. For a less spicy soup, leave the chilies whole.

• For tom yam soup with chicken, substitute boneless, skinless chicken breast for shrimp. Cut chicken into thin strips and cook until just opaque throughout, 1–2 minutes. Continue as above.

Tomato rasam

Serves 8–10

1 cup (7 oz/220 g) split yellow lentils

3½ qt (3.5 L) water

1 teaspoon ground turmeric

¼ teaspoon powdered asafoetida

1 tablespoon vegetable oil

3 tomatoes, about ¾ lb (12 oz/375 g) total, unpeeled, coarsely chopped

1½ teaspoons tamarind concentrate

2 teaspoons crushed garlic

1½ tablespoons rasam masala (see below)

⅓ cup (¾ oz/20 g) chopped fresh cilantro (fresh coriander)

juice of ½ lemon

18 fresh curry leaves, torn into small pieces

salt to taste

Place lentils in a sieve and rinse under cold running water. Drain well. In large, heavy saucepan, combine lentils, water, turmeric, asafoetida and oil. Bring to a boil then reduce heat to medium–low and cook, uncovered, until lentils are mushy, about 30 minutes.

Add tomatoes, tamarind and garlic to cooked lentils. Simmer, uncovered, until tomatoes break down, 20–25 minutes.

Stir in rasam masala, cilantro, lemon juice and curry leaves. Season with salt. Serve hot.

For rasam masala

1¼ cups coriander seeds

¼ cup dried red chilies broken into small pieces

1½ tablespoons cumin seeds

1 teaspoon black mustard seeds

1 teaspoon black peppercorns

¼ cup firmly packed fresh curry leaves

¼ teaspoon powdered asafoetida

In a small saucepan over low heat, separately dry-roast coriander, chilies, cumin, mustard and peppercorns until fragrant and only lightly colored. Place roasted spices in a bowl. Dry-roast curry leaves in pan, tossing, until crisp. Add to spices with asafoetida. Mix well and let cool. Just before using rasam masala, grind to a powder in a spice grinder.

Tip

Rasam masala can be kept in an airtight jar and stored in refrigerator for up to 6 months.

Vegetable and lentil soup

Serves 4

3 tablespoons peanut oil

2 tablespoons peeled and grated fresh ginger

1 small red chili, seeded and finely sliced

¼ teaspoon ground cumin

¼ teaspoon curry powder

1 small red (Spanish) onion, chopped

1 small parsnip, peeled and sliced

2 celery stalks, thinly sliced

4 large carrots, peeled and sliced

1 potato, peeled and sliced

2 fresh kaffir lime leaves or ¼ teaspoon grated lime zest (rind)

½ cup (3½ oz/105 g) red or brown lentils

6 cups (48 fl oz/1.5 L) vegetable stock (see page 222)

1 cup (8 fl oz/250 ml) coconut milk

2 tablespoons chopped fresh cilantro (fresh coriander), for garnish

In a large saucepan over medium heat, warm peanut oil. Add ginger, chili, cumin and curry powder and cook until aromatic, about 1 minute. Add onion, parsnip, celery, carrots, potato and lime leaves. Cover and cook, stirring occasionally, for 10 minutes. Add lentils and stock and bring to a boil. Cover and cook until vegetables and lentils are soft, about 20 minutes. Remove lime leaves and discard.

Working in batches, puree soup in a food processor. Return to saucepan, add coconut milk and heat through, about 3 minutes. Garnish with chopped cilantro and serve.

Tip

Bird's eye and serrano chilies are recommended for this recipe.

Vegetable laksa

Serves 4

4 tablespoons light olive oil

2 small red chili, finely chopped

3 cloves garlic, finely chopped

2-inch (5-cm) piece fresh ginger, peeled and grated

1 stalk lemongrass, bottom 3 inches (7.5 cm) only, finely chopped

1 teaspoon ground coriander

1/2 teaspoon turmeric

1 teaspoon dark brown sugar

1/4 cup (2 fl oz/60 ml) lime juice

3 cups (24 fl oz/750 ml) coconut milk

3 cups (24 fl oz/750 ml) vegetable stock (see page 222) or chicken stock (see page 218)

4 medium yellow tomatoes, cut into quarters

8 oz (250 g) fresh thick rice noodles

2 medium Asian eggplants (aubergines), cut diagonally into 1-inch (2.5-cm) pieces

1 small green bell pepper (capsicum), seeded and cut into thin strips

1 small yellow bell pepper (capsicum), seeded and cut into thin strips

5 oz (150 g) bean sprouts

1/4 cup (2 fl oz/60 g) crispy fried shallots (French shallots) (see Seafood Laksa, page 66)

In a large saucepan over medium–high heat, heat 2 tablespoons oil. Add chilies, garlic, ginger, lemongrass, coriander, turmeric and brown sugar and cook, stirring, until mixture is fragrant, 3–4 minutes. Add lime juice, coconut milk and stock. Increase heat to high and bring liquid to a steady simmer. Reduce heat to medium and simmer for 15 minutes. Add tomatoes and cook for 5 minutes.

Bring a large saucepan of water to a boil. Add noodles and cook until tender, about 3 minutes. Drain noodles and set aside. In a heavy-bottomed frying pan over medium–high heat, heat remaining oil. Add eggplant slices in a single layer and cook until golden and cooked through, 3–4 minutes on each side.

Rinse noodles under very hot water, using a fork to separate them, and place in individual bowls. Ladle soup over noodles and top with eggplant, bell peppers, bean sprouts and crispy fried shallots.

Vegetable pho

Serves 4

6 cups (48 fl oz/1.5 L) vegetable stock (see page 222)

6 cloves

4 black peppercorns

2-inch (5-cm) piece fresh ginger, peeled and sliced

1 cinnamon stick

2 star anise

4 cardamom pods

1 tablespoon fish sauce

8 oz (250 g) green beans, sliced

8 oz (250 g) thick asparagus spears, cut into 2-inch (5-cm) pieces

8 oz (250 g) dried rice noodles

6 oz (180 g) chopped Chinese greens, such as bok choy or choy sum, or English spinach

4 sprigs fresh mint

4 sprigs fresh cilantro (fresh coriander)

chili sauce, for serving

fish sauce, for serving

lime wedges, for serving

In a large saucepan over medium–high heat, combine stock, spices and fish sauce and bring to a steady simmer. Simmer until stock is infused with flavor, about 20 minutes. Strain through a fine sieve. Discard solids, return stock to saucepan over medium heat and simmer gently.

Bring a small saucepan of water to a boil. Add beans and asparagus and cook for 2 minutes. Drain, then set aside.

Place noodles in a bowl and cover with boiling water. Let stand until soft, about 5 minutes. Drain noodles and place in individual bowls. Top noodles with Chinese greens, cooked beans and asparagus, and mint and cilantro sprigs. Ladle stock into bowls.

Serve immediately, accompanied by chili sauce, fish sauce and lime wedges for each diner to add according to taste.

chicken and duck

1 teaspoon salt, plus extra salt to taste

2½ tablespoons grated fresh ginger

2½ tablespoons crushed garlic

2 teaspoons chili powder

3 teaspoons ground turmeric

2 teaspoons chopped fresh green chilies

2 lb (1 kg) tomatoes, about 7 medium, chopped and pureed in blender or food processor

⅔ cup (5 fl oz/150 ml) heavy (double) cream

¼ cup (2 oz/60 g) unsalted butter

4 teaspoons honey

2 tablespoons dried fenugreek leaves

⅓ cup (½ oz/15 g) chopped fresh cilantro (fresh coriander)

Butter chicken

Serves 4–6

2 lb (1 kg) chicken thigh fillets

¼ cup (2 fl oz/60 ml) white vinegar or lemon juice

⅓ cup coriander seeds

2-inch (5-cm) cinnamon stick, broken into smaller pieces

5 brown or black cardamom pods

10 green cardamom pods

1 teaspoon whole cloves

3 teaspoons ground turmeric

2 teaspoons chili powder

2 teaspoons paprika

1 teaspoon ground nutmeg

1 teaspoon ground mace

¼ cup (2 oz/60 g) plain (natural) whole-milk yogurt

2½ tablespoons crushed garlic

2½ tablespoons grated fresh ginger

2½ tablespoons vegetable oil

salt to taste

For sauce

½ cup (4 fl oz/125 ml) vegetable oil and melted unsalted butter combined

2 lb (1 kg) yellow (brown) onions, about 6 medium, chopped

Cut chicken fillets into quarters. In a glass or ceramic bowl, combine chicken with 4 teaspoons vinegar or lemon juice and turn to coat. Set aside.

In a spice grinder, grind coriander seeds, cinnamon, cardamom and cloves to a powder. Place in a bowl and combine with turmeric, chili powder, paprika, nutmeg, mace, remaining vinegar or lemon juice, yogurt, garlic, ginger and oil, and mix well. Season with salt and add to chicken. Mix well, cover and place in refrigerator to marinate for 30 minutes.

Preheat oven to 475°F (240°C/Gas 9). Oil a shallow roasting pan and place chicken pieces in pan in a single layer. Bake, without turning, for 12 minutes. Remove from oven and set aside.

To make sauce: In a deghchi or large frying pan, heat oil and butter mixture over medium–low heat. Add onions and 1 teaspoon salt and cook, uncovered, stirring occasionally, until onions are dark golden brown, about 15–20 minutes. Add ginger and garlic and cook, stirring, for 2 minutes. Add chili powder, turmeric and chilies, and cook for 1 minute. Add tomatoes and cook, uncovered, stirring often, until tomatoes are soft, about 5–10 minutes.

Add cream and butter to pan, and cook, stirring, until butter melts. Stir in chicken, honey and fenugreek, and cook, stirring often, until chicken is cooked through, about 5 minutes. Stir in cilantro. Taste and add salt if necessary. Serve immediately.

Chicken and noodles in crisp lettuce cups

Serves 4

2 Chinese dried mushrooms

3½ oz (105 g) cellophane (bean thread) noodles

1 tablespoon vegetable oil

2 small red chilies, seeded, if desired, and
   chopped

2 cloves garlic, crushed

12 oz (375 g) ground (minced) chicken

6 scallions (shallots/spring onions), sliced

¼ cup (1 oz/30 g) finely chopped canned bamboo
   shoots

¼ cup (2 oz/60 g) finely chopped canned water
   chestnuts

juice of 1 lime

2 tablespoons fish sauce

2 tablespoons chopped fresh mint

3 tablespoons chopped fresh cilantro (fresh coriander)

1 tablespoon Asian sesame oil

1 small head butter or iceberg lettuce, leaves
   separated and trimmed

Thai sweet chili sauce, for serving

Place mushrooms in small bowl, add boiling water to cover and let stand for 10–15 minutes. Drain and squeeze out excess liquid. Finely chop mushrooms, discarding tough stems.

Soak noodles in boiling water for 10 minutes. Drain and set aside.

In a frying pan over medium–high heat, warm vegetable oil. Add chilies and garlic and cook until aromatic, about 1 minute. Add ground chicken and mushrooms and cook, stirring occasionally, until chicken is browned, 4–5 minutes. Remove from heat and stir in noodles, scallions, bamboo shoots, water chestnuts, lime juice, fish sauce, mint, cilantro and sesame oil. Mix well.

To serve, arrange lettuce leaves on individual plates. Spoon chicken mixture on leaves. Drizzle with chili sauce.

Chicken and nut curry

Serves 4

For spice paste

1 onion, coarsely chopped

⅓ cup (3 fl oz/80 ml) tomato paste

⅓ cup (2 oz/60 g) roasted cashew nuts

2 teaspoons garam masala (see page 223)

3 cloves garlic, chopped

1 tablespoon fresh lemon juice

1 teaspoon grated lemon zest

¼ teaspoon ground turmeric

1 teaspoon sea salt

1 tablespoon plain (natural) yogurt

2 tablespoons vegetable oil

3 oz (90 g) dried apricots

1 lb (500 g) skinless, boneless chicken thighs, cut
    into strips ⅜-inch (1-cm) wide

1¼ cups (10 fl oz/300 ml) chicken stock (see page 218)

¼ cup (1½ oz/45 g) roasted cashew nuts for garnish

¼ cup (¼ oz/7 g) fresh cilantro (fresh coriander)
    leaves for garnish

To make spice paste: In a food processor, combine all
ingredients and process until smooth, about 30 seconds.
Transfer to a small bowl.

In a wok or large skillet, heat oil over medium heat and
fry spice paste until fragrant, about 2 minutes. Add
apricots and chicken. Cook for 1 minute. Stir in stock,
cover, and simmer over low heat until chicken is tender,
10–12 minutes. Spoon into serving bowls. Garnish with
cashews and cilantro leaves. Serve with steamed
basmati rice.

Chicken chettinad

Serves 4–6

2 lb (1 kg) chicken thigh fillets, cut into 1-inch (2.5-cm)
  pieces
½ cup (4 fl oz/125 ml) buttermilk
⅔ cup (5 fl oz/150 ml) vegetable oil and melted
  unsalted butter combined
1-inch (2.5-cm) cinnamon stick
3 green cardamom pods, cracked
3 whole cloves
1 teaspoon powdered asafoetida
5 yellow (brown) onions, chopped
2½ tablespoons crushed fresh ginger
2½ tablespoons crushed garlic
3–4 teaspoons chili powder
2½ tablespoons ground coriander
4 teaspoons ground turmeric
salt to taste
8 tomatoes, chopped
1 cup (1½ oz/45 g) chopped fresh cilantro (coriander)
2 tablespoons crushed black peppercorns
18 fresh curry leaves
steamed basmati rice

In a glass or ceramic bowl, combine chicken and
buttermilk, and mix well. Place in refrigerator to marinate
while preparing sauce.

In a large, heavy saucepan or karhai, heat oil and butter
mixture over medium heat. Add cinnamon, cardamom and
cloves and cook until fragrant, about 30 seconds.
Immediately stir in asafoetida, then add onions. Cook
onions, uncovered, stirring often, until dark golden brown,
10–15 minutes. Add ginger and garlic and cook, stirring, for
1 minute. Add chili powder, coriander, turmeric and salt to
taste, and stir until fragrant, about 1 minute. Add tomatoes
and cook, uncovered, stirring occasionally, until tomatoes
soften and sauce thickens slightly, 10–15 minutes.

Stir in chicken and buttermilk and cook, stirring often, until
chicken is cooked through, 5–10 minutes. Add cilantro,
peppercorns and curry leaves and mix well. Serve with
steamed rice.

Chicken curry

Serves 4

2 tablespoons vegetable oil

3 bay leaves

4 whole cardamom pods, bruised

1 tablespoon coriander seeds, crushed

2 teaspoons chili flakes

1 onion, chopped

1 tablespoon peeled and grated fresh ginger

4 cloves garlic, finely chopped

1 large fresh red Thai or Anaheim chili, seeded and
chopped

1 large fresh green Thai or Anaheim chili, seeded and
chopped

4 tomatoes, peeled and chopped

1 lb (500 g) boneless, skinless chicken breast halves,
cut into bite-sized pieces

1½ cups (12 fl oz/375 ml) coconut milk

1 tablespoon green peppercorns

2 tablespoons chopped fresh cilantro (fresh coriander)

In a wok or skillet, heat oil over medium heat and fry bay
leaves, cardamom, coriander, chili flakes, onion, ginger,
garlic, and chilies until onion is soft, 2–3 minutes. Stir in
tomatoes and cook until tomatoes are split, about
3 minutes. Add chicken and fry until chicken becomes
opaque, 4–6 minutes. Add coconut milk and peppercorns.
Reduce heat and simmer until chicken is tender, 5–6
minutes. Remove from heat and stir in cilantro. Serve with
steamed basmati rice.

Chicken with ginger

Serves 4–6

1 cup (2 oz/60 g) cloud or tree ear mushrooms (black or white fungus)

¼ cup (2 fl oz/60 ml) vegetable oil

6 cloves garlic, coarsely chopped

1 small onion, thinly sliced

12 oz (375 g) boneless, skinless chicken breasts, thinly sliced

1 cup (4 oz/125 g) loosely packed, julienned fresh ginger, preferably young ginger

1 tablespoon fish sauce

3 tablespoons oyster sauce

1 tablespoon soy sauce

1 tablespoon soybean paste

2 fresh long red chilies, cut into large pieces

½ cup (4 fl oz/125 ml) chicken stock (see page 218) or water

8 scallions (shallots/spring onions), white part only, chopped

If using dried mushrooms, soak in water for 10 minutes; drain. Use scissors to trim hard core, then cut mushrooms into pieces.

In a wok or large, heavy frying pan over high heat, heat oil and fry garlic just until it starts to brown. Immediately add onion and chicken and stir-fry until meat is opaque on all sides, about 2 minutes.

Add ginger and mushrooms, then fish sauce, oyster sauce, soy sauce and soybean paste. Stir-fry for 1 minute. Add chilies and stock or water, bring to a boil and cook for 1 minute. Stir in scallions.

Transfer to a serving dish and serve.

Tip

If cloud or tree ear mushrooms are unavailable, substitute an equal quantity of straw mushrooms or standard mushrooms.

Chicken with lemongrass and chili

Serves 6

1½ lb (750 g) chicken thighs

1 tablespoon fish sauce

salt and white pepper

2 lemongrass stalks, trimmed and finely chopped

2 scallions (shallots/spring onions), trimmed and
   finely chopped

3 tablespoons vegetable oil

1 cup (8fl oz/250 ml) water

2 fresh red chilies, seeded and sliced

1 teaspoon crumbled palm or brown sugar

Cut the chicken portions in half, though the bone. Use a sharp skewer to prick chicken, to allow seasonings to penetrate. Place in a dish and pour on fish sauce, sprinkle on seasonings and leave for 15 minutes.

In a large frying pan or wok, heat oil and brown chicken evenly. Stir in the lemongrass, onions and water. Cover and cook until the chicken is almost tender, about 15 minutes, turning several times.

Add chilies and sugar and cook a further 5–7 minutes. The liquid should evaporate, leaving chicken free of sauce. Serve over rice.

Chicken vindaloo

Serves 4

For marinade

²/₃ cup (5 fl oz/160 ml) malt vinegar

1½ teaspoons coriander seeds, crushed

1 teaspoon cumin seeds, crushed

1 teaspoon chili powder

¼ teaspoon ground turmeric

3 cloves garlic, finely chopped

1 teaspoon peeled and grated fresh ginger

1 teaspoon sea salt

1½ teaspoons sweet paprika

1 tablespoon tomato paste

pinch ground fenugreek

1¼ cups (10 fl oz/300 ml) water

1 lb (500 g) skinless, boneless chicken breast halves, cut into 1-inch (2.5-cm) cubes

1 tablespoon vegetable oil

1 onion, sliced

6 fresh curry leaves

1 large potato, peeled and cut into 1-inch (2.5-cm) cubes

2 green Thai or Anaheim chilies, seeded and finely chopped

To make marinade: In a baking dish, combine all ingredients and stir to blend. Add chicken and toss to coat. Cover and refrigerate for 30 minutes.

In a wok or large skillet, heat oil over medium heat and fry onion and curry leaves until onions are soft, about 1 minute. Reduce heat, add chicken and marinade, and fry for 2 minutes. Add potato, cover and simmer until potato and chicken are tender, about 10 minutes. Remove from heat and stir in green chilies.

Tip

This is a traditional hot Indian curry, so serve with steamed basmati rice or naan.

Chili chicken

Serves 4–6

3-inch (8-cm) cinnamon stick

2 teaspoons green cardamom pods

2 teaspoons whole cloves

1 teaspoon black peppercorns

1/3 cup (3/4 oz/20 g) chopped fresh cilantro (fresh
    coriander)

36 fresh curry leaves

juice of 1 lemon

4 teaspoons finely chopped fresh green chilies

4 teaspoons finely grated fresh ginger

4 teaspoons crushed garlic

2 teaspoons tamarind concentrate

1 teaspoon ground turmeric

salt to taste

2 lb (1 kg) chicken thigh fillets, quartered

2 tablespoons vegetable oil

Preheat oven to 475°F (240°C/Gas 9). In a spice grinder,
grind cinnamon, cardamom, cloves and peppercorns to a
powder. Transfer spices to a food processor and add
cilantro, curry leaves, lemon juice, chilies, ginger, garlic,
tamarind, turmeric and salt. Process to form a paste.

Place chicken pieces in a glass or ceramic bowl and add
spice mixture. Mix well to coat chicken and set aside to
marinate for 10–15 minutes.

Brush vegetable oil over a large baking sheet and spread
coated chicken on sheet in a single layer. Bake, without
turning, until chicken is cooked through, about 20 minutes.
Serve immediately.

Tip

Serve the chicken with a salad made from 1 diced onion
and 2 diced scallions (shallots/spring onions).

Duck and green chili curry

Serves 4

For spice paste

2 fresh green Thai or Anaheim chilies, coarsely
  chopped
1 onion, coarsely chopped
2 teaspoons ground turmeric
1 tablespoon ground coriander
1 tablespoon raw cashew nuts
2 teaspoons peeled and grated fresh ginger
4 cloves garlic, coarsely chopped
2 black peppercorns
2 tablespoons water

3 tablespoons vegetable oil
2 bay leaves
1 stalk lemongrass, white part only, bruised
1/2 teaspoon dried shrimp paste
1 lb (500 g) boneless duck or chicken breasts, with
  skin, cut into 1-inch (2.5-cm) cubes
1 cup (8 fl oz/250 ml) water
1 tablespoon tamarind paste
16 fresh basil leaves

To make spice paste: In a food processor, combine all ingredients and process to a thick paste. Scrape into a small bowl.

In a wok or large skillet, heat 2 tablespoons oil over medium heat and fry spice paste until fragrant, about 1 minute. Add bay leaves, lemongrass and shrimp paste. Stir-fry for 1 minute, add duck or chicken and stir-fry until opaque, 4–5 minutes. Stir in 1 cup 8 fl oz/250 ml) water, reduce heat to a simmer and cook until duck is tender, about 15 minutes. Remove from heat and stir in tamarind paste. Remove lemongrass.

In a small skillet, heat remaining 1 tablespoon oil over medium heat and fry basil leaves in batches. Using a slotted spoon, transfer to paper towels to drain. Spoon curry into serving bowls and garnish each serving with fried basil leaves. Serve with steamed basmati rice.

Duck on a bed of chili onions

Serves 4

4 tablespoons chili oil (see page 220)

19 oz (590 g) yellow (brown) onions, thinly sliced

3 cloves garlic, finely chopped

1 small red chili, seeded and sliced

4 duck or chicken breasts, 4–5 oz (125–150 g) each

1 tablespoon ground ginger

1 tablespoon ground coriander

1 tablespoon ground black pepper

1 teaspoon sea salt

2 tablespoons vegetable oil, for frying

4 oz (125 g) sugar snap peas

¼ cup (¼ oz/7 g) loosely packed, small, fresh Thai
basil leaves

Thai sweet chili sauce, for serving (optional)

Preheat oven to 225°F (110°C/Gas ¼). In a frying pan over medium–low heat, warm 2 tablespoons chili oil. Add onions, garlic and chili and cook until onions are transparent and soft, about 10 minutes. Transfer to a heatproof dish and keep warm in preheated oven.

Using tip of a sharp knife, score skin side of each duck breast. In a small bowl, combine ginger, coriander, pepper and salt. Brush breasts with remaining 2 tablespoons chili oil. Rub breasts with spice mixture. In a frying pan over medium heat, warm vegetable oil. Add duck breasts and cook until golden and cooked through, 5–6 minutes per side. Remove from pan, place on a heatproof dish and keep warm in oven.

Bring a saucepan of water to a boil. Remove from heat, add sugar snap peas and cook for 1 minute. Immediately drain and rinse under cold running water. Drain.

Spoon onions onto plates. Cut each duck breast diagonally into 4–6 slices. Arrange slices over onions and garnish with basil. Serve with sugar snap peas and Thai sweet chili sauce.

Festive duck curry

Serves 4

1 tablespoon peeled and grated fresh ginger

4 cloves garlic, finely chopped

2 tablespoons rice vinegar

1 lb (500 g) boneless duck breast fillets, with skin,
  cut into strips ¼-inch (6-mm) wide

2 tablespoons vegetable oil

1 onion, chopped

2 teaspoons ground cumin

2 teaspoons ground coriander

1 teaspoon chili powder

2 tomatoes, peeled and chopped

1 cup (8 fl oz/250 ml) chicken stock (see page 218)

1 tablespoon fish sauce

1 teaspoon ground pepper

2 tablespoons chopped fresh cilantro (fresh
  coriander)

In a small bowl, combine ginger, garlic and vinegar. Put duck in a baking dish. Add ginger mixture and toss until well coated. Cover and refrigerate for 1 hour.

In a wok or large skillet, heat oil over medium heat and fry onion until soft, about 1 minute. Add cumin, coriander and chili powder. Fry for 1 minute. Add duck and marinade. Fry until duck is opaque, 4–5 minutes. Add tomatoes and stir-fry for 3 minutes. Stir in stock, fish sauce and pepper. Reduce heat to low, cover and simmer until duck is tender, 10–12 minutes. Stir in cilantro. Spoon into serving bowls. Serve with steamed jasmine rice.

Green curry with chicken

Serves 4–6

2 cups (16 fl oz/500 ml) coconut milk

1–2 tablespoons vegetable oil (optional)

¼ cup (2 fl oz/60 ml) green curry paste (see page 227)

12 oz (375 g) boneless, skinless chicken breasts,
 thinly sliced

½ cup (2 oz/60 g) chopped eggplant (aubergine) or
 3 round Thai eggplants

¼ cup (1 oz/30 g) pea eggplants (optional)

2 tablespoons palm sugar (optional)

2 fresh kaffir lime leaves, stemmed

½ cup (1/2 oz/15 g) loosely packed, fresh sweet Thai
 basil leaves

2 tablespoons fish sauce

1 fresh long green chili, cut into large pieces

1 fresh long red chili, cut into large pieces

Let coconut milk stand, allowing the thick coconut milk
to rise to the top. Spoon thick coconut milk into a small
bowl and reserve 2 tablespoons of this for garnish.

In a wok or large, heavy frying pan, heat thick coconut
milk over medium–high heat, stirring constantly, until it
separates, 3–5 minutes. If it does not separate, add
optional oil. Add green curry paste and fry, stirring
constantly, until fragrant, about 2 minutes.

Add chicken and cook until meat is opaque on all sides,
2–3 minutes. Add remaining thin coconut milk and
bring to a boil. Add both the eggplants and simmer until
slightly soft, about 4 minutes. If desired, add palm sugar
to taste. Tear kaffir lime leaves and basil into pieces. Stir
in fish sauce, lime leaves and half the basil.

Remove from heat and transfer to a serving bowl. Drizzle
over reserved 2 tablespoons coconut cream. Garnish
with green and red chilies and remaining basil leaves
and serve.

Tip

To make green curry with shrimp, substitute an equal
amount of shelled and deveined jumbo shrimp (king
prawns), with tails attached. Add raw shrimp soon after
the eggplants and cook briskly for 2 minutes. If using
raw shrimp, make sure the liquid is boiling when adding
them, lest they turn mushy. Cooked shrimp should be
added only during final minute of cooking to heat
through.

Grilled coconut chicken

Serves 4

1¼ cups (10 fl oz/300 ml) thin coconut cream or
　coconut milk

3 cloves garlic, finely chopped

2 small red chilies, seeded and finely chopped

1 teaspoon freshly grated ginger

½ cup (1 oz/30 g) fresh cilantro (fresh coriander)
　leaves

grated zest (rind) and juice of 1 lime

3 tablespoons soy sauce

1 tablespoon fish sauce

1 tablespoon grated palm sugar or brown sugar

4 chicken breast fillets, with skin

1 tablespoon vegetable oil

1 bunch (13 oz/400 g) bok choy, rinsed and cut in
　half lengthwise

In a food processor or blender, combine coconut cream, garlic, chilies, ginger, cilantro, rind, juice, soy sauce, fish sauce and sugar. Process until smooth, about 30 seconds, to make marinade.

Place chicken fillets onto a cutting board and make 3 slits in skin side of each fillet using a sharp knife. Place chicken into a shallow nonmetallic dish. Pour marinade ingredients over chicken and cover dish with plastic wrap. Refrigerate for 2 hours. Drain chicken, reserving marinade.

Preheat a grill pan or barbecue, then brush grill lightly with oil. Grill chicken until tender, 4–5 minutes each side. Test chicken by piercing the thickest part with a skewer; chicken is cooked if juices run clear. Remove from grill.

Meanwhile, steam or blanch bok choy in a saucepan of boiling water until tender crisp, about 2 minutes. Place reserved marinade ingredients into a small saucepan. Stir over medium heat and bring to a boil. Boil for 1 minute, remove from heat and set aside. To serve, arrange bok choy on serving plates and top each with a chicken fillet. Drizzle with warm marinade. Serve any extra marinade in a separate serving dish.

Lime chicken and pork patties

Serves 4

1 lb (500 g) ground (minced) chicken thigh meat

8 oz (250 g) ground (minced) lean pork meat

8 scallions (shallots/spring onions), chopped

3 cloves garlic, finely chopped

3 small red chilies, 1 seeded and finely
  chopped, 2 seeded and sliced

¼ cup (⅓ oz/10 g) finely chopped fresh cilantro
  (fresh coriander) leaves

2 teaspoons grated fresh kaffir lime zest (rind)

2 tablespoons fresh kaffir lime juice

1½ cups (3 oz/90 g) fresh white breadcrumbs

1 egg, beaten

2 tablespoons vegetable oil

12 fresh basil leaves

1 baby Romaine (cos) lettuce, leaves separated and
  washed, for serving

In a large mixing bowl, combine chicken, pork, scallions, garlic, chopped chilies, cilantro, zest, juice, breadcrumbs and egg. Using wet hands, mix until well combined. Divide into 12 portions and shape each into a round patty. Place in a single layer on a plate, cover with plastic wrap and refrigerate for 1 hour.

Preheat a grill pan or barbecue, then brush grill lightly with oil. Grill patties until golden and tender, 2–3 minutes each side. Remove from grill. In a small saucepan, warm leftover vegetable oil and fry basil leaves and sliced chilies until aromatic, about 1 minute.

To serve, place chicken patties onto serving plates with lettuce leaves and top each with fried basil and chili slices.

Penang duck curry

Serves 2

¼ cup (2 fl oz/60 ml) coconut cream

1½ tablespoons Thai red curry paste (see page 227)

3 fresh kaffir lime leaves

½ cup (2½ oz/75 g) fresh or frozen green peas

2 teaspoons fish sauce

2 teaspoons packed brown sugar

1½ cups (12 fl oz/375 ml) coconut milk

½ Chinese roast duck, cut into serving pieces

¼ cup (¼ oz/7 g) fresh basil leaves

In a large saucepan or wok, heat coconut cream over medium heat until oil separates from cream. Stir in curry paste and cook until fragrant, about 1 minute. Add lime leaves and peas and cook for 1 minute. Stir in fish sauce, brown sugar, coconut milk and duck. Stir over medium heat until duck is heated through, 3–4 minutes. Spoon into serving bowls and top with basil leaves. Serve with steamed jasmine rice.

Poached chicken in green coconut sauce

Serves 4

2½ cups (20 fl oz/625 ml) coconut milk

2 tablespoons green curry paste (see page 227)

3 fresh kaffir lime leaves or 1 teaspoon grated lime
  zest (rind)

1 tablespoon fish sauce

1 long green chili, halved

1 lb (500 g) skinless chicken thigh fillets, cut into
  1-inch (2.5-cm) cubes

steamed jasmine rice, for serving

¼ cup (¼ oz/7 g) fresh cilantro (fresh coriander)
  leaves, for garnish

In a saucepan over low heat, combine coconut milk,
curry paste, lime leaves, fish sauce and chili. Stir until
heated through, about 5 minutes; do not boil. Add
chicken and cook, stirring, until tender, about 20
minutes. Serve hot with steamed jasmine rice. Garnish
with cilantro leaves.

Spicy chicken skewers with mint yogurt

Serves 2

1 lb (500 g) chicken breast fillets

3 teaspoons ground coriander

2 teaspoons ground turmeric

1 small red chili, seeded and finely chopped

4 cloves garlic, finely chopped

2 tablespoons superfine (caster) sugar

1 teaspoon sea salt

12 bamboo skewers

2 tablespoons peanut oil

6½ oz (200 g) choy sum or other Asian greens, coarsely chopped

For mint yogurt

½ cup (4 fl oz/125 ml) plain (natural) yogurt

2 cloves garlic, finely chopped

2 tablespoons chopped fresh mint leaves

¼ cup (1½ oz/40 g) peeled, seeded and chopped cucumber

Cut chicken fillets into 1½-inch (4-cm) cubes. In a small bowl, combine ground coriander, turmeric, chili, garlic, sugar and salt. In a bowl, toss chicken pieces in spice mixture. Cover bowl with plastic wrap and refrigerate for 2 hours. Soak bamboo skewers in water for 10 minutes, then drain. Thread chicken pieces onto bamboo skewers.

Preheat a grill pan or barbecue, then brush grill with oil. Grill chicken skewers until golden and tender, 2–3 minutes each side.

Steam or blanch choy sum in boiling water until tender crisp, about 3 minutes, then drain. Serve chicken warm with mint yogurt and steamed choy sum.

To make mint yogurt: In a small bowl, combine yogurt, garlic, mint and cucumber. Mix until well combined. Cover and chill before serving.

Spicy oven-roasted chicken

Serves 4

1 chicken, about 3 lb (1.5 kg)

1/2 teaspoon saffron threads

1 tablespoon boiling water

6 cloves garlic, crushed

2 tablespoons peeled and grated fresh ginger

1/3 cup (3 fl oz/90 ml) fresh lemon juice

1/2 teaspoon ground chili

2 teaspoons ground paprika

1 teaspoon salt

3 teaspoons garam masala (see page 223)

olive oil cooking spray

steamed jasmine rice, for serving

Preheat oven to 350°F (180°C/Gas 4). Rinse and dry chicken. Truss chicken with kitchen string.

In a small bowl, combine saffron and boiling water and soak for 10 minutes.

In a food processor or blender, combine saffron mixture, garlic, ginger, lemon juice, chili, paprika, salt and garam masala. Process until smooth. Rub spice mixture over chicken. Cover and refrigerate for 2–3 hours, or as long as overnight.

Spray chicken lightly with cooking oil spray. Place in an oiled roasting pan and cook until golden and tender and juices run clear when chicken is pierced with a sharp knife, about 1 1/4 hours. Serve hot or cold with steamed jasmine rice.

Star anise and roasted duck risotto

Serves 4–6

½ Chinese roast duck

6 cups (48 fl oz/1.5 L) chicken stock (see page 218)

3 star anise

2-inch (5-cm) piece fresh ginger

4 tablespoons olive oil

6 scallions (shallots/spring onions), white and pale
   green parts, finely sliced

5 oz (150 g) fresh shiitake mushrooms, sliced

1 small red bell pepper (capsicum), seeded and
   chopped

1⅓ cups (9 oz/280 g) arborio rice

Remove meat and skin from duck and discard bones.
Cut meat and skin into bite-sized pieces, about 1½
inches (4 cm). Cover and refrigerate until ready to use.

In a saucepan, combine stock, star anise and ginger and
bring to a boil. Reduce heat to simmer, cover and
cook for 20 minutes. Strain stock into another
saucepan and discard star anise and ginger. Bring
stock to a simmer over low heat.

In a saucepan over medium heat, warm 2 tablespoons
olive oil. Add scallions, mushrooms and bell pepper
and cook until mushrooms soften, 2–3 minutes.
Transfer mushroom mixture to a bowl and set aside.

In a saucepan over medium heat, warm remaining
2 tablespoons olive oil. Add rice and cook, stirring
constantly, until rice grains are evenly coated with oil,
about 2 minutes. Add 1 cup (8 fl oz/250 ml) hot stock
to rice, reduce heat to simmer and cook, stirring
constantly, until liquid is absorbed. Add remaining
stock, 1 cup (8 fl oz/250 ml) at a time, continuing to
stir constantly, until rice is al dente and creamy. Add
duck and mushroom mixture and stir gently until
heated through. Serve immediately.

Tandoori chicken

Serves 4

4 chicken legs

4 chicken thighs

¾ cup (6 oz/180 g) plain (natural) yogurt

1 teaspoon garam masala (see page 223)

2 teaspoons peeled and grated fresh ginger

6 cloves garlic, finely chopped

¼ teaspoon ground turmeric

1 teaspoon ground coriander

1 tablespoon fresh lemon juice

¼ teaspoon Chinese powdered red food coloring

pinch of sea salt

1 tablespoon vegetable oil

2 limes, quartered

Using a sharp knife, make 2 slits in skin side of each chicken piece. Place chicken pieces in a baking dish. In a small bowl, combine yogurt, garam masala, ginger, garlic, turmeric, coriander, lemon juice, red coloring, salt and oil. Mix well. Pour over chicken pieces and toss to coat chicken. Cover and refrigerate for 2 hours.

Remove chicken from refrigerator 30 minutes before roasting. Preheat oven to 425°F (220°C/Gas 7). Transfer chicken to a roasting pan. Roast until juices run clear when the chicken is pierced with a sharp knife, about 25 minutes. Remove from oven. Serve immediately, with lime wedges.

Tip

Tandoori chicken is traditionally cooked on a spit in a clay tandoor oven, but you can also prepare it in a regular oven.

Thai basil chicken

Serves 4

5 oz (150 g) cellophane (bean thread) noodles or rice
 vermicelli
2 tablespoons fish sauce
1 tablespoon rice wine
5 cloves garlic, crushed
2 tablespoons finely chopped scallions
 (shallots/spring onions)
1 lb (500 g) skinless chicken breast fillets, sliced
2 tablespoons vegetable oil
1 small red chili, seeded, if desired, and
 chopped
1 red bell pepper (capsicum), seeded and sliced
1 red (Spanish) onion, sliced
2 tablespoons soy sauce
1 tablespoon water
2 teaspoons palm sugar or brown sugar
½ cup (½ oz/15 g) fresh basil leaves

Soak noodles in boiling water for 10 minutes; drain. In a
bowl, combine fish sauce, rice wine, 2 cloves garlic and
scallions. Add chicken and stir to coat with marinade.
Cover and allow to marinate in refrigerator for 1 hour.
Drain.

In a wok or frying pan over medium–high heat, warm oil.
Add remaining 3 cloves garlic and chili. Cook until
aromatic, about 1 minute. Add chicken and cook until
tender, 4–5 minutes. Reduce heat to medium and stir in
bell pepper, onion, noodles, soy sauce, water and sugar.
Cook, stirring occasionally, until noodles are heated
through, about 2 minutes. Remove from heat and stir in
basil.

Spoon into individual bowls and serve immediately.

Thai chicken and pumpkin curry

Serves 4

For spice paste

½ teaspoon chili flakes

1 teaspoon ground coriander

¼ teaspoon ground cumin

¼ teaspoon ground turmeric

½ teaspoon ground cinnamon

¼ teaspoon ground cloves

¼ teaspoon ground star anise

2 cardamom pods, bruised

1 scallion (shallot/spring onion), chopped

1 teaspoon finely chopped fresh cilantro (fresh coriander) roots

2 cloves garlic, finely chopped

1-inch (2.5-cm) piece fresh galangal, peeled and finely chopped

2 fresh kaffir lime leaves, shredded

sea salt to taste

2 tablespoons vegetable oil

2 cloves garlic, finely chopped

1½ cups (12 fl oz/375 ml) coconut milk

½ cup (4 fl oz/125 ml) chicken stock (see page 218)

2 teaspoons fish sauce

1½ cups (8 oz/250 g) cubed, peeled pumpkin or butternut squash

1 lb (500 g) skinless, boneless chicken thighs, cut into strips ⅜-inch (1-cm) wide1 onion, sliced lengthwise

½ cup (3 oz/90 g) unsalted roasted peanuts

1 tablespoon packed brown sugar

3 fresh kaffir lime leaves, shredded

3 tablespoons tamarind paste

½ fresh red Thai or Anaheim chili, seeded and cut into 1½-inch (4-cm) shreds

To make spice paste: In a small skillet, combine chili flakes, coriander, cumin, turmeric, cinnamon, cloves, star anise and cardamom pods. Stir over medium heat until fragrant, about 1 minute. Transfer to a food processor and add remaining ingredients. Process to a smooth paste.

In a wok or large skillet, heat oil over medium heat. Add garlic and spice paste and fry until fragrant, 1–2 minutes. Stir in coconut milk and stock, reduce heat and simmer for 3 minutes. Add fish sauce and pumpkin. Cover and simmer for 5 minutes. Add chicken and simmer until chicken and pumpkin are tender, 5–6 minutes. Add onion, peanuts, brown sugar, lime leaves and tamarind paste. Simmer for 1 minute. Spoon into serving bowls and garnish with shredded chili. Serve with steamed jasmine rice.

Thai spicy chicken with basil

Serves 4

2 tablespoons vegetable oil

2 teaspoons Asian sesame oil

3 cloves garlic, finely chopped

1 tablespoon peeled and grated fresh ginger

4 small red chilies, halved and seeded

1 red bell pepper (capsicum), seeded and sliced

1 lb (500 g) skinless chicken thigh fillets, cut into
  1-inch (2.5-cm) cubes

2 tablespoons soy sauce

2 tablespoons water

2 teaspoons brown sugar

½ cup (½ oz/15 g) fresh basil leaves

6 scallions (shallots/spring onions), cut diagonally
  into 1-inch (2.5-cm) lengths

steamed jasmine rice, for serving

In a wok or frying pan over medium heat, warm vegetable and sesame oils. Add garlic, ginger and chilies and cook until aromatic, about 1 minute. Raise heat to high, add bell pepper and chicken and stir-fry until chicken is golden, about 5 minutes. Stir in soy sauce, water and brown sugar. Reduce heat to medium and cook until chicken is cooked through, about 5 minutes. Stir in basil and scallions. Spoon into bowls and serve with steamed jasmine rice.

beef, lamb and pork

Balti beef

Serves 4

2 tablespoons ghee or vegetable oil

1 onion, chopped

1 teaspoon grated fresh ginger

1 teaspoon paprika

1 teaspoon turmeric

1 teaspoon garlic puree

1 tablespoon curry paste

1 cup (8 fl oz/250 ml) beef stock

salt and freshly ground black pepper

1½ lb (700 g) rib-eye steak, cut into small thin slices

8 oz (225 g) small okra, trimmed

15 oz (425 g) canned chickpeas, drained

9 oz (250 g) fresh young English spinach

2 teaspoons garam marsala (see page 223)

2 teaspoons dried fenugreek leaves

4 naan breads, for serving

In a small pan, heat 1 tablespoon ghee. Add onion and ginger and cook until onion is soft, 2–3 minutes. Add paprika and turmeric, cook for 1 minute, then stir in garlic puree, curry paste, stock, salt and pepper. Bring to a boil then simmer, uncovered, until liquid has been reduced to half, about 10 minutes.

In a large frying pan or wok, heat remaining ghee. Stir-fry beef and okra for about 2 minutes to seal the meat. Add chickpeas, spinach and curry sauce and mix well. Cook gently until spinach has wilted and chickpeas are heated through. Stir in garam marsala and fenugreek leaves.

Divide between four warmed serving dishes and eat with naan bread.

Beef and bamboo shoots

Serves 4

2 fresh bamboo shoots (about 10 oz/300 g each)

5 cups (40 fl oz/1.25 L) rice water (reserved after
washing rice)

1 dried red chili

vegetable or sunflower oil, for frying

2 oz (60 g) Korean watercress stems (minari)

3 dried Chinese mushrooms, soaked for 30 minutes in
several changes of water

4 oz (125 g) beef tenderloin or scotch fillet, thinly
sliced into strips about 1½ inches (4 cm) long

4 oz (125 g) bean sprouts, trimmed

1 egg, separated

1 medium red chili pepper, julienned into 1½-inch
(4-cm) strips

For beef and mushroom marinade

2 tablespoons light soy sauce

1 tablespoon sugar

2 teaspoons crushed garlic

2 teaspoons Asian sesame oil

2 teaspoons pan-toasted, ground sesame seeds

4 teaspoons finely chopped scallions (shallots/spring
onions)

freshly ground black pepper to taste

For seasoning

2 teaspoons light soy sauce

2 teaspoons table salt

2 teaspoons sugar

1 tablespoon white vinegar

2 teaspoons pan-toasted, ground sesame seeds

Slice bamboo shoots diagonally into 1½-inch (4-cm)
pieces. In a large saucepan, bring rice water to a
simmer. Add bamboo shoots and dried chili, and simmer
uncovered for 1 hour. Remove bamboo shoots from
water and set aside to cool. Peel and slice in half
lengthwise. In a frying pan over medium heat, heat
2 tablespoons oil and fry bamboo shoot slices for
3–5 minutes. Repeat process to fry watercress stems,
omitting dried chili.

Squeeze excess water from mushrooms. Remove and
discard stems and cut caps into thin slices.

To make beef and mushroom marinade: In a large glass
or ceramic bowl, combine marinade ingredients. Add
beef and mushrooms and mix well to coat. In a frying
pan, heat 1 tablespoon oil and stir-fry beef and
mushrooms for 3–5 minutes.

Bring a small saucepan of salted water to a boil.
Immerse bean sprouts in boiling water for a few
seconds. Remove and drain.

Fry egg white and yolk separately, tilting pan to create a
pancake round of each. Remove from pan and slice
each thinly. Reserve a few slices for garnish.

To make seasoning: Combine all ingredients in a large
bowl. Add all ingredients to seasoning, mix well to coat,
then add chili strips. Transfer to a large platter, decorate
with reserved egg slices and serve with steamed rice.

Beef and long bean curry

Serves 6

3 lb (1½ kg) braising beef (flank, shin, round etc.), cut
  into 1¼-inch (3-cm) cubes
2 tablespoons vegetable oil
4 cups (32 fl oz/1 L) thin coconut milk
1 large onion, coarsely chopped
3–4 tablespoons red curry paste (see page 227)
1 tablespoon coriander seeds
¾ lb (375 g) Chinese long (snake) beans or green
  beans
salt and pepper, to taste
lime juice, to taste
fresh cilantro (fresh coriander) sprigs
1 fresh red chili, seeded and shredded

Place beef and coconut milk in a saucepan. Bring to a boil
and simmer for 10 minutes, then drain, reserving coconut
milk.

In the same pan, heat the oil and sauté onion until lightly
browned. Add curry paste and cook, stirring continually,
for about 5 minutes. Pour in coconut milk and bring to a
boil. Reduce heat and allow sauce to simmer for about
25 minutes.

Meanwhile, toast coriander seeds in a pan without oil, or
in a hot oven, then grind finely. Add to sauce.

Return meat and simmer, covered, for 1 hour. It may be
necessary to add a little more liquid (either water or
coconut milk) as the dish should have a generous amount
of sauce.

Top and tail beans and cut into 2-inch (5-cm) lengths. Add
to curry and cook until beans and meat are tender.
Season to taste with salt and pepper, and add a dash of
lime juice to heighten the taste.

Transfer to a serving dish and garnish with cilantro sprigs
and chili shreds. Serve with jasmine rice, or aromatic,
long-grain rice such as basmati, garnished with sprigs of
fresh herbs.

Beef rendang

Serves 4

1 onion, coarsely chopped

6 cloves garlic

1 tablespoon peeled and grated fresh ginger

1 teaspoon chili powder

3 teaspoons ground turmeric

3 teaspoons ground coriander

1 tablespoon coconut milk

1 tablespoon vegetable oil

3 whole cloves

1 cinnamon stick

1¼ lb (625 g) lean beef, cut into 1-inch (2.5-cm) cubes

2 cups (16 fl oz/500 ml) extra coconut milk

2 tablespoons tamarind paste

1 teaspoon packed brown sugar

sea salt to taste

In a food processor, combine onion, garlic, ginger, chili powder, turmeric, coriander and coconut milk and process to a smooth paste.

In a wok or large skillet, heat oil over low heat and stir-fry cloves and cinnamon until fragrant, about 1 minute. Add spice paste and cook for 1 minute. Add beef and cook until beef changes color on all sides, 4–5 minutes. Stir in extra coconut milk and bring to a boil. Reduce heat to low and simmer until beef is tender, 15–20 minutes. Add tamarind, sugar and salt. Spoon into serving bowls. Serve with steamed basmati rice.

Beef tagine with couscous

Serves 4

1 teaspoon ground ginger

1 teaspoon ground cinnamon

½ teaspoon ground allspice

pinch of ground cloves

1½ lb (700 g) lean braising steak (chuck or blade),
  cut into chunks

1 tablespoon olive oil

1 onion, sliced

1 clove garlic, crushed

grated zest (rind) and juice of 1 lemon

2 tablespoons quince jelly or honey

1 cup (8 fl oz/250 ml) prune juice

1 teaspoon harissa or sambal oelek (see page 228)
  or cayenne pepper to taste

salt and freshly ground black pepper

For couscous

2½ cups (20 fl oz/600 ml) water

8 oz (225 g) couscous

2 tablespoons olive oil

1 onion, chopped

1 teaspoon ground cinnamon

½ teaspoon ground allspice

1 teaspoon ground turmeric

1 tablespoon ground cumin

1 teaspoon ground coriander

1 teaspoon dried mint

⅓ cup (3 oz/85 g) pistachio nuts

⅓ cup (3 oz/85 g) pine nuts

fresh cilantro (fresh coriander) leaves, for garnish

Preheat oven to 325°F (170°C/Gas 3). Mix together ginger, cinnamon, allspice and cloves and rub into beef.

In a heavy-based casserole, heat oil and cook onion and garlic until soft. Add beef and cook until beef is browned, 2–3 minutes. Add lemon zest and juice, quince jelly, prune juice, harissa and salt and pepper, and bring to a boil. Transfer to oven and cook until meat is tender, 1¼ hours.

When meat has been in the oven for about ½ hour, prepare couscous. Boil water and pour into a large bowl with couscous. Let stand until all the water is absorbed, about 10 minutes.

In a frying pan, heat oil and fry onion until soft. Add remaining ingredients, except cilantro, stir well and cook for 2–3 minutes. Add onion to couscous and mix well. Transfer couscous to a lightly greased ring tin or spread over a serving plate. Cover with aluminum foil and put into bottom of oven until meat is cooked.

Remove couscous from oven and turn out onto a serving plate. Spoon beef into middle of couscous if using a ring tin or onto a separate plate if not, and garnish with cilantro.

Beef vindaloo

Serves 4–6

5 dried red chilies, broken into small pieces

1 teaspoon cumin seeds

1 tablespoon black peppercorns

1½ tablespoons finely grated fresh ginger

1½ tablespoons crushed garlic

½ teaspoon ground turmeric

¾ cup (6 fl oz/180 ml) vegetable oil and melted
   unsalted butter combined

1½ lb (750 g) yellow (brown) onions, about 4½
   medium, finely chopped

1 teaspoon salt, plus extra salt to taste

2 lb (1 kg) beef chuck, excess fat removed, cut into
   1½-inch (4-cm) pieces

about 4 cups (32 fl oz/1 L) water

4 fresh green chilies, slit lengthwise

½ cup (4 fl oz/125 ml) white vinegar

½ teaspoon tamarind concentrate

½ teaspoon sugar

steamed basmati rice, for serving

In a spice grinder, grind dried chilies, cumin seeds and
peppercorns to a powder. Place in a bowl and combine
with ginger, garlic and turmeric. Set aside.

In a karhai or frying pan, heat oil and butter mixture over
medium–low heat. Add onions and 1 teaspoon salt, and
cook, uncovered, stirring often, until onions are dark
golden brown, 20–25 minutes. Raise heat to
medium–high and add beef. Cook, turning beef pieces,
for 5 minutes. Add spice mixture and cook, stirring, until
fragrant, about 2 minutes.

Pour in enough water to cover beef. Add fresh chilies and
bring to a simmer. Cook over low heat, partially covered,
stirring occasionally, until liquid is reduced by half, about
1 hour.

Stir in vinegar, tamarind and sugar. Taste and add salt if
necessary. Cook, uncovered, until sauce reduces and
thickens, about 30 minutes. Serve hot with steamed rice.

Braised pork with young coconut

Serves 6

1½ lb (750 g) boneless pork shank, leg or shoulder,
cut into 1-inch (2.5-cm) cubes

⅓ cup (3 oz/90 g) sugar

2 coconuts, preferably young coconuts, or about
4 cups (32 fl oz/1 L) coconut water (see Tips
opposite)

2 tablespoons vegetable oil

⅔ cup (5 fl oz/150 ml) fish sauce

6 hard-boiled eggs, shelled

1 fresh long red or green chili, seeded and thinly
sliced

⅓ cup (½ oz/15 g) coarsely chopped Chinese
(flat/garlic) chives

6 scallions (shallots/spring onions), including green
parts, cut into 1-inch (2.5-cm) pieces

Place pork in a medium casserole dish. Sprinkle with
sugar and refrigerate for 1 hour. Traditionally, any rind is
retained to enrich the juices, but discard if preferred.

Pierce top of coconuts and drain coconut water; you need
about 4 cups (32 fl oz/1 L). If using young coconuts, use a
large knife to cut away the top of the coconut (the shell of
young coconuts is not as hard as that of older ones).
Scoop gelatinous flesh from inside shell and cut into small
dice; set aside.

In a medium pot, heat oil over medium heat and cook
pork, stirring, until lightly golden on all sides, 3–5 minutes.
You may need to do this in 2 batches to prevent
crowding. If meat begins to burn because of sugar, add
1–2 tablespoons coconut water. Add fish sauce and
remaining coconut water, and, if using, coconut meat.
Bring to a low boil, then immediately reduce heat to low,
partially cover, and very gently simmer until pork is tender
and liquid reduced by half, about 2–2½ hours. Add hard-
cooked eggs to the pot for last 30 minutes of cooking
time. Serve garnished with chili, chives and scallions.

Tips

• This is a southern Vietnamese recipe, popularly sold on
the streets of Ho Chi Minh City (Saigon). Cook very slowly
to ensure tender results.

• Coconut water is not coconut milk, but the watery liquid
inside a coconut. While coconut water from older
coconuts can be used, try to find young coconuts or
packaged coconut water. Often, the water is lightly
sweetened. If so, omit sugar. Alternatively, the separated
clear liquid layer in canned coconut milk can be used.
(See also page 219.)

Chili beef burgers with Asian salad

Serves 4

1 lb (500 g) ground (minced) lean beef

1 clove garlic, crushed

1 small red chili, seeded and finely chopped

1 small yellow (brown) onion, grated

2 tablespoons chopped fresh cilantro (fresh coriander)

1 tablespoon vegetable oil, for brushing

4 cups (4 oz/125 g) arugula (rocket)

20 fresh Vietnamese mint leaves

½ cup (¾ oz/20 g) loosely packed fresh cilantro
   (fresh coriander) leaves

1 tablespoon chili oil (see page 220)

salt and freshly ground black pepper

4 crusty rolls, halved

¼ cup (2 fl oz/60 ml) Thai sweet chili sauce (optional)

In a bowl, combine beef, garlic, chili, onion and cilantro. Using wet hands, mix well. Divide into 4 portions and shape each portion into a patty, flattening it slightly to fit size of roll.

Heat a frying pan over high heat. Brush both sides of beef patties with vegetable oil and fry until cooked through to center, 3–4 minutes per side.

In a bowl, combine arugula, mint and cilantro. Drizzle with chili oil and season with salt and pepper. Place greens on bottom halves of rolls. Add beef patties and drizzle with Thai sweet chili sauce if desired. Add tops of rolls and serve.

Coconut beef curry

Serves 4

1 tablespoon vegetable oil

1 tablespoon Asian sesame oil

1 onion, chopped

1 tablespoon peeled and grated fresh ginger

5 cloves garlic, finely chopped

1 tablespoon ground turmeric

1 teaspoon chili powder

1 lb (500 g) lean beef, cut into 1-inch (2.5-cm) cubes

1 stalk lemongrass, white part only, bruised

1 cup (8 fl oz/250 ml) water

1 cup (8 fl oz/250 ml) coconut milk

6 oz (185 g) green beans, trimmed and halved
   crosswise

2 tablespoons chopped fresh cilantro (fresh coriander)

In a wok or large skillet, heat oils over medium heat and fry onion, ginger, and garlic until fragrant, about 1 minute. Add turmeric and chili powder and fry for 30 seconds. Add beef and cook until beef changes color, 3–4 minutes. Add lemongrass, water and coconut milk. Bring to a boil, reduce heat to low and simmer until beef is tender, 10–15 minutes. Add beans and cook for 3 minutes. Remove from heat and stir in cilantro. Spoon into serving bowls. Serve with steamed basmati rice.

Fried pork with green onions

Serves 4

4¹⁄₂ teaspoons salt

1 tablespoon ginger juice (obtained by grating fresh ginger)

2 tablespoons rice wine

10 oz (300 g) pork tenderloin, cut into pieces 1¹⁄₂ inches (4 cm) wide by 2 inches (5 cm) long

¹⁄₄ cup (1 oz/30 g) cornstarch (cornflour)

2 cups (16 fl oz/500 ml) vegetable or sunflower oil, for deep-frying

3 cloves garlic, peeled and finely sliced

1 fresh red chili, seeds removed, cut into 1¹⁄₄-inch (3-cm) strips

3 scallions (shallots/spring onions), cut into 2-inch (5-cm) lengths

2 tablespoons light soy sauce

2 tablespoons malt liquid (mullyeot)

freshly ground black pepper

Asian sesame oil to taste

lettuce leaves, for serving

In a medium-sized glass or ceramic bowl, combine salt, ginger juice and rice. Add pork pieces, cover and refrigerate to marinate for 2–3 hours. Remove pork pieces from marinade and coat with cornstarch.

In a wok or deep frying pan over high heat, heat oil. Add pork cubes one at a time so they do not stick together and fry for 1 minute. Remove from oil and drain on paper towels.

In a wok or frying pan over medium heat, heat 1 tablespoon oil and stir-fry garlic and chili for 2 minutes. Add pork and continue stir-frying for 3–5 minutes. Add scallions, soy sauce, malt liquid and pepper and stir-fry for 1 minute. Sprinkle with sesame oil. Arrange lettuce leaves on a large plate, spoon fried pork into center and serve.

Green curry pork

Serves 4

1 tablespoon vegetable oil

3 tablespoons Thai green curry paste (see page 227)

1 lb (500 g) lean pork, cut into 1-inch (2-cm) cubes

1 tablespoon green peppercorns

4 fresh green bird's eye or Thai chilies

2 tablespoons peeled and finely shredded fresh
   galangal

1 cup (8 fl oz/250 ml) coconut milk

2 teaspoons fish sauce

2 teaspoons packed brown sugar

4 fresh kaffir lime leaves

In a wok or large skillet, heat oil over medium heat and fry
curry paste until fragrant, about 30 seconds. Add pork,
and stir-fry until pork changes color, about 2 minutes. Stir
in all remaining ingredients. Reduce heat to low and
simmer until pork is tender, 12–15 minutes. Spoon into
serving bowls. Serve with steamed jasmine rice.

Jungle curry with pork

Serves 4–6

¼ cup (2 fl oz/60 ml) vegetable oil
¼ cup (2 fl oz/60 ml) red curry paste (see page 227)
12 oz (375 g) boneless pork butt or loin, thinly sliced
¼ cup (1 oz/30 g) chopped eggplant (aubergine)
¼ cup (1 oz/30 g) pea eggplants (optional)
2 long beans or 8 green beans, cut into 1-inch
  (2.5-cm) pieces
½ cup (2 oz/60 g) julienned krachai (Chinese keys)
¼ cup fresh green peppercorns on stem, or
  1–2 tablespoons canned green peppercorns, drained
6 ears (cobs) fresh or canned baby corn, rinsed and
  drained, cut into large pieces
2 cups (16 fl oz/500 ml) chicken stock or water
5 fresh kaffir lime leaves, stemmed
½ cup (½ oz/15 g) loosely packed, fresh Thai basil
  leaves, preferably holy basil
¼ teaspoon salt
2 tablespoons fish sauce
1 fresh long red chili, cut into large pieces

In a wok or large, heavy frying pan over medium–high heat, heat oil. Add curry paste and fry, stirring constantly, for 1–2 minutes. Add pork and stir-fry until it changes color on all sides, about 2 minutes.

Add eggplants, beans, krachai, peppercorns, corn and 1 cup (8 fl oz/250 ml) stock or water. Bring to a boil, stirring often, then simmer, uncovered, for 2 minutes. Add the remaining stock, increase heat and bring to a boil.

Tear kaffir lime leaves and basil into pieces. Stir lime leaves, salt, fish sauce and chili into the curry. Boil for 1 minute. Add basil leaves and immediately remove from heat. Transfer to a serving dish and serve.

Tip

Replace pork with an equal quantity of beef or chicken. Traditionally, wild boar is used in this recipe.

Korean beef rolls

Serves 4

vegetable oil, for deep-frying, plus 1 tablespoon
3½ oz (105 g) cellophane (bean thread) noodles or rice
  vermicelli
4 cloves garlic, crushed
1 tablespoon peeled and grated fresh ginger
1 small red chili, seeded, if desired, and
chopped, or 1 teaspoon chili paste
12 oz (375 g) lean ground (minced) beef
¼ cup (1 oz/30 g) chopped scallions (shallots/spring
  onions)
2 teaspoons Asian sesame oil
5 oz (150 g) firm tofu, finely chopped
12 butter lettuce leaves, trimmed
12 scallions (shallots/spring onions), blanched
  (optional)
Thai sweet chili sauce, for serving

In wok or frying pan, heat vegetable oil until it reaches
375°F (190°C) on a deep-frying thermometer or until a
small bread cube dropped in oil sizzles and turns golden.
Working in small batches, add noodles and fry until crisp,
about 30 seconds. Using a slotted spoon, remove from
pan and drain on paper towels.

In a wok or frying pan over medium–high heat, warm
1 tablespoon vegetable oil. Add garlic, ginger and chili and
stir-fry until aromatic, approximately 1 minute. Add ground
beef and cook, stirring, until meat changes color, 3–4
minutes. Stir in chopped scallions, sesame oil and tofu
and cook 1 minute.

Place a lettuce leaf on a work surface. Spoon small
amount of crisp noodles and beef mixture on leaf. Roll up;
tie with blanched scallion if desired. Repeat with remaining
lettuce leaves.

Divide rolls among individual plates, placing them seam-
side down, and accompany with Thai sweet chili sauce.
Alternatively, the ingredients can be served in separate
bowls, and guests can assemble their own rolls.

Lamb and potato rissoles

Serves 4 (makes 12)

2 teaspoons good-quality curry powder

½ teaspoon sea salt

1 tablespoon white vinegar

1 tablespoon ghee

2 cloves garlic, finely chopped

1 teaspoon peeled and grated fresh ginger

1 onion, chopped

6 oz (185 g) ground (minced) lamb

½ cup (4 fl oz/125 ml) hot water

1 teaspoon garam masala (see page 223)

2 tablespoons chopped fresh cilantro (fresh
coriander)

1 tablespoon chopped fresh mint

extra ½ onion, chopped

2½ lb (1.25 kg) potatoes, peeled and chopped

1 teaspoon sea salt

2 tablespoons chopped fresh mint

3 scallions (shallots/spring onions), chopped

1 fresh green Thai or Anaheim chili, seeded and
chopped

1 egg, beaten

1½ cups (6 oz/185 g) dried bread crumbs

3 cups (24 fl oz/750 ml) vegetable oil, for deep-frying

In a small bowl, stir curry powder, salt and vinegar together to make a paste. In a wok or large skillet, melt ghee and fry garlic, ginger, and chopped onion until onion is soft, 1–2 minutes.

Stir in curry powder, salt and vinegar. Mix well. Stir in lamb, increase heat to high, and cook until meat changes color, 2–3 minutes. Reduce heat to low, cover and cook until liquid is absorbed. Remove from heat. Add garam masala, cilantro, mint, and ½ chopped onion. Transfer to a bowl and let cool completely.

Cook potatoes in salted boiling water until tender, 8–12 minutes. Drain and mash. Add salt, mint, scallions and chili. Stir well to blend. Form into 12 patties. Place

1 tablespoonful of meat filling in the center and close potato mixture around filling. Dip in beaten egg, then bread crumbs to coat evenly. Cover and refrigerate for 30 minutes.

In a wok, Dutch oven, or deep fryer, heat oil to 375°F (190°C), or until a small bread cube dropped in the oil sizzles and turns golden in 1 minute. Fry rissoles in batches until golden, 2–3 minutes. Using a slotted spoon, transfer to paper towels to drain. Serve hot.

Lamb biryani

Serves 4–6

4 yellow (brown) onions, halved and thinly sliced

1 teaspoon salt, plus extra salt to taste

1 cup (8 fl oz/250 ml) vegetable oil and melted
unsalted butter combined

1¼ cups (10 oz/300 g) plain (natural) whole-milk
yogurt

1 cup (1½ oz/45 g) chopped fresh cilantro (fresh
coriander)

1 cup (1½ oz/45 g) chopped fresh mint

6 fresh green chilies, chopped

1½ tablespoons finely grated fresh ginger

1½ tablespoons crushed garlic

1½ tablespoons garam masala (see page 223)

2 tablespoons chili powder

1½ tablespoons ground turmeric

2 lb (1 kg) boneless lamb shoulder, diced

pinch saffron threads soaked in 2 tablespoons hot
milk for 10 minutes

2 lb (1 kg) basmati rice, rinsed and soaked in cold
water to cover for 20 minutes

juice of 1 lemon

herb yogurt dip (see page 223), for serving

Preheat oven to 475°F (240°C/Gas 9). In a bowl,
combine onions with 1 teaspoon salt. Set aside for 10
minutes. In large deghchi or large, deep ovenproof
saucepan, heat oil and butter mixture over medium–low
heat. Add onions and cook, uncovered, stirring often,
until onions are dark golden brown, 20–25 minutes.
Strain onions and reserve oil and butter mixture. Let
onions cool slightly.

In a large glass or ceramic bowl, combine yogurt,
cilantro, mint, chili, ginger, garlic, garam masala, chili
powder and turmeric. Season with salt. Add cooked
onions, lamb, and saffron mixture, and mix well. Spread
lamb mixture in base of deghchi or saucepan.

Drain rice and place in a large saucepan with enough
boiling water to cover. Season with salt. Bring to a boil
over high heat and cook, uncovered, for 7 minutes.
Drain excess water from rice. Spread rice evenly over
lamb mixture. Pour reserved oil and butter mixture evenly
over rice. Cover tightly with lid. "Scrunch" a long piece of
aluminum foil around top edge of deghchi or saucepan
to create a seal.

Place deghchi or saucepan over medium–high heat for
5 minutes, then transfer to oven. Reduce oven
temperature to 400°F (200°C/Gas 6) and cook for
40 minutes. Remove from oven and let stand
15 minutes before removing seal and lid. Either serve
from pan or place a large platter over deghchi or
saucepan and then very carefully invert biryani onto
platter. (You will need two people to do this). Serve
immediately drizzled with lemon juice and accompanied
by herb yogurt dip.

Lamb roganjosh

Serves 4–6

2 lb (1 kg) lamb shoulder, diced

2 cups (1 lb/500 g) plain (natural) whole-milk yogurt, whisked

1 teaspoon salt, plus extra salt to taste

²/₃ cup (5 fl oz/150 ml) vegetable oil and melted unsalted butter combined

1-inch (2.5-cm) cinnamon stick

20 green cardamom pods

5 brown or black cardamom pods

1 teaspoon whole cloves

2 lb (1 kg) yellow (brown) onions, about 6 medium, chopped

2 tablespoons finely grated fresh ginger

2 tablespoons crushed garlic

4 teaspoons chili powder

2 teaspoons ground turmeric

¹/₃ cup (¹/₂ oz/15 g) chopped fresh cilantro (fresh coriander)

1¹/₂ teaspoons garam masala (see page 223)

steamed basmati rice or paratha bread, for serving

In a large bowl, combine lamb, yogurt and ¹/₂ teaspoon salt and mix well. Set aside for 10 minutes.

In a large karhai or frying pan, heat oil and butter mixture over medium heat. Add cinnamon, cardamom and cloves, and cook, stirring, until fragrant, about 30 seconds. Add onions and ¹/₂ teaspoon salt and cook over medium–low heat, uncovered, stirring often, until onions are golden brown, 20–25 minutes.

Add ginger and garlic and cook, stirring, for 30 seconds. Drain away any excess oil and butter, leaving onions and spices in pan.

Add lamb and yogurt mixture, chili powder and turmeric to pan and mix well. Cook over low heat, covered, until lamb is tender, 45–60 minutes. Add cilantro and garam masala and mix well. Taste and add salt if necessary. Serve hot with steamed rice or paratha.

Massaman curry with lamb

Serves 4–6

2 cups (16 fl oz/500 ml) coconut milk

2–3 tablespoons vegetable oil (optional)

¼ cup (2 fl oz/60 ml) massaman curry paste (see page 226)

12 oz (375 g) boneless lamb leg, thinly sliced

2 potatoes, or 12 oz (375 g) sweet potato, taro, or pumpkin, peeled and cubed

1 teaspoon palm sugar

5 bay leaves

5 cardamom pods, toasted

2–3 tablespoons fish sauce

3–5 tablespoons tamarind puree, to taste

adjat sauce (see page 216), for serving

Let coconut milk stand, allowing the thick coconut milk to rise to the top. Spoon thick coconut milk into a small bowl, and reserve 2 tablespoons for garnish.

In a wok or large, heavy frying pan, heat the thick coconut milk over medium–high heat, stirring constantly, until it separates, 3–5 minutes. If it does not separate, add optional oil. Add curry paste and fry, stirring constantly, until fragrant, 1–2 minutes.

Add meat and potatoes or other vegetable and cook until lamb is lightly browned on both sides, 2–3 minutes. Add remaining thin coconut milk, increase heat and bring to a boil. Add palm sugar—if using a wok, add it along the edge of the wok so that it melts before stirring into the curry; if using a frying pan, add directly to the curry. Add remaining ingredients and bring just to a boil.

Reduce heat and simmer until vegetables are tender, about 20 minutes. Transfer to a serving bowl, and serve with adjat sauce.

Tips

• Massaman curry is named after Thailand's Moslem minority living in the south and is consequently never made with pork. It is popular throughout the kingdom.

• For Massaman curry with beef, substitute an equal amount of cubed beef chuck, round (topside) or blade steak for the lamb. Tougher meat cuts may require thinner slicing and longer simmering.

Mini chili tomato meatballs with udon noodles

Serves 4

1 lb (500 g) ground (minced) beef

1 large onion, finely chopped

1 clove garlic, crushed

2½ tablespoons tomato paste

2 tablespoons Worcestershire sauce

2 tablespoons chopped fresh parsley

1 small red chili, seeded and finely chopped

1 egg, lightly beaten

salt and freshly ground pepper

25 oz (780 g) fresh udon noodles

¼ teaspoon salt

2 tablespoons olive oil

For tomato sauce

1 tablespoon olive oil

2 scallions (shallots/spring onions), chopped

1 clove garlic, crushed

3 large tomatoes, peeled and coarsely chopped

2 teaspoons soy sauce

1 tablespoon lemon juice

2 teaspoons Worcestershire sauce

1 tablespoon chopped fresh basil or thyme

salt and cracked black pepper to taste

1 small red chili, seeded and finely chopped, (optional)

2 tablespoons chopped fresh parsley, for garnish

In a medium bowl, combine beef, onion, garlic, tomato paste, Worcestershire sauce, parsley, chili, egg, salt and pepper and mix well. Line a large bamboo steamer or steamer basket with parchment (baking) paper. With wet hands, take about 1 tablespoon mixture at a time and shape into small balls, and place in a single layer in steamer.

Partially fill a pot or wok with water (steamer should not touch water) and bring to a rapid simmer. Place steamer over water, cover and steam until meatballs are cooked, 8–10 minutes. Add noodles and salt to water for the last 6 minutes of cooking, or until noodles are just tender. Drain noodles and toss with olive oil to keep from sticking.

To make tomato sauce: While meatballs are cooking, heat oil in a medium saucepan over medium–low heat. Add scallions and garlic and cook until soft but not brown, about 5 minutes. Reduce heat, stir in remaining ingredients, except chili and parsley, cover, and cook until thick, about 10 minutes. If a thinner sauce is preferred, add a little chicken stock. Add the chili if desired.

Divide noodles among four plates and serve topped with meatballs and sauce and sprinkled with parsley.

Moroccan lamb tagine with apricots

Serves 4

2 tablespoons all-purpose (plain) flour

salt and freshly ground pepper

1½ lb (750 g) lamb from leg or shoulder, cut into
   1-inch (2½-cm) cubes

3 tablespoons olive oil

1 onion, sliced

1 teaspoon ground coriander

1 teaspoon ground cumin

½ teaspoon ground cardamom

½ teaspoon cardamom seeds

2 cloves garlic, crushed

3 cups (24 fl oz/750 ml) chicken stock (see page 218)

¾ cup (4 oz/125 g) dried apricots

½ lemon, thinly sliced

8 fresh apricots, halved and pitted

¼ cup (⅓ oz/10 g) chopped fresh parsley, for
   garnish

2 cups (12 oz/315 g) instant couscous

salt

2 cups (16 fl oz/500 ml) boiling water

3 tablespoons butter (optional)

Place flour and salt and pepper to taste in a plastic bag. Add lamb pieces and shake until pieces are coated. In a large heavy saucepan over medium–high heat, heat 2 tablespoons oil. Add lamb pieces, in batches, and cook, stirring, until browned on all sides, 3–4 minutes. Drain lamb on a plate lined with paper towels.

In pan over medium heat and add onion, heat remaining 1 tablespoon oil. Cook until soft, about 5 minutes. Add spices and garlic and cook 1 minute. Return meat to pan and add stock and dried apricots. Bring to a boil and simmer, uncovered, stirring occasionally, for 1 hour.

Add lemon slices and fresh apricots and simmer until apricots are tender, about 10 minutes. Season to taste with salt and ground pepper.

Place couscous in a large bowl. Lightly salt boiling water and pour over couscous. Cover immediately and let stand, uncovered, for 10 minutes. Remove cover and fluff grains with fork. Stir in butter if desired.

Serve lamb with couscous. Sprinkle with parsley.

Pork curry on noodles

Serves 4

8 oz (250 g) lean ground (minced) pork

4 cloves garlic, crushed

2 lemongrass stalks, chopped, or grated zest (rind) of 1 lemon

1 tablespoon peeled and grated fresh ginger

1 tablespoon vegetable oil

1 tablespoon green curry paste (see page 227), or to taste

1½ cups (12 fl oz/375 ml) coconut milk

1 cup (8 fl oz/250 ml) chicken stock (see page 218)

2 tablespoons fish sauce

2 teaspoons palm sugar or brown sugar

8 oz (250 g) hokkien noodles

½ cup (¾ oz/20 g) fresh basil leaves, plus basil leaves, for serving

4 scallions (shallots/green onions), chopped

¼ cup (⅓ oz/10 g) chopped fresh cilantro (coriander)

In a bowl, combine ground pork, garlic, lemongrass or lemon zest and ginger. Using moistened hands, mix until well combined. Shape into walnut-size balls.

In a wok or frying pan over medium–high heat, warm oil. Add curry paste and cook until aromatic, about 1 minute. Stir in coconut milk and stock. Reduce heat to low and simmer gently for 3 minutes. Raise heat to medium and add pork balls, fish sauce and sugar. Cook, stirring occasionally, until pork changes color, about 5 minutes.

Cook noodles as directed on package or on page 23. Drain.

Arrange noodles in individual soup or pasta bowls. Stir ½ cup (¾ oz/20 g) basil leaves, scallions and cilantro into curry. Spoon over noodles and garnish with fresh basil leaves. Serve immediately.

Pork with ginger and lime sauce

Serves 4

3 tablespoons fresh lime juice

2 teaspoons peeled and grated fresh ginger

2 cloves garlic, finely chopped

2 tablespoons honey

2 tablespoons soy sauce

3 tablespoons dry sherry

salt and freshly ground black pepper

4 butterfly pork chops, about 3½ oz (105 g) each

1 lb (500 g) pumpkin or butternut squash, peeled, seeded, and cut into 2-inch (5-cm) pieces

¼ cup (⅓ oz/10 g) chopped fresh cilantro (fresh coriander) leaves

3 tablespoons vegetable oil

In a shallow glass or ceramic dish, combine lime juice, ginger, garlic, honey, soy sauce, sherry and salt and pepper to taste. Add pork and turn to coat with marinade. Cover and refrigerate for 30 minutes.

Bring a saucepan of water to a boil. Add squash and cook until soft, 8–10 minutes. Drain, place in a bowl and mash with a fork or potato masher. Add cilantro and stir to combine. Season with salt and pepper.

Preheat oven to 225°F (110°C/Gas ¼).

Remove pork chops from marinade, reserving marinade. Pat pork dry with paper towels. In a frying pan over medium heat., warm vegetable oil. Add pork and cook until tender, 3–4 minutes per side. Remove from pan, place on a heatproof plate and keep warm in preheated oven. Add reserved marinade to pan, bring to a boil and cook for
1 minute. Divide squash among individual plates. Top with pork, drizzle with warm pan juices and serve.

Red hot beef

Serves 4

2 stalks lemongrass
1 large red chili, seeded and chopped
1 teaspoon grated fresh ginger
2 cloves garlic
1 teaspoon ground coriander
1 teaspoon ground cumin
grated rind (zest) and juice of 1 lime
1 tablespoon paprika
1 teaspoon chili powder
1 cup (8 fl oz/250 ml) coconut cream
2 tablespoons sunflower oil
1½ lb (700 g) lean braising steak (chuck, blade or
  shin), diced
salt
2 onions, thinly sliced
2 red bell peppers (capsicums), seeded and thinly
  sliced
lime slices, for garnish
fresh cilantro (fresh coriander) leaves, for garnish

Preheat oven to 325°F (170°C/Gas 3). In a blender or food processor, combine lemongrass, chili, ginger, garlic, coriander, cumin, lime zest and juice, paprika, chili powder and coconut cream. Process until smooth.

In a frying pan, heat 1 tablespoon oil and fry beef until brown. Transfer to a heavy-based ovenproof dish, stir in spice mixture, season with salt, cover and cook in oven until very tender, about 1½ hours.

In the same frying pan, heat remaining 1 tablespoon oil and cook onion and bell peppers until soft. Stir into meat.

Transfer to a warm serving dish and garnish with lime and cilantro.

Spicy lamb

Serves 4

1 tablespoon vegetable oil

4 cardamom pods

1 cinnamon stick

4 whole cloves

1 onion, finely chopped

12 oz (375 g) ground (minced) lamb

2 teaspoons garam masala (see page 223)

1 teaspoon chili powder

4 cloves garlic, finely chopped

3 teaspoons peeled and grated fresh ginger

1 teaspoon sea salt

6 oz (185 g) potatoes, peeled and cut into 1-inch (2.5-cm) cubes

13 oz (390 g) canned chopped tomatoes

½ cup (4 fl oz/125 ml) hot water

2 tablespoons chopped fresh cilantro (fresh coriander)

2 tablespoons chopped fresh mint

In a wok or large skillet, heat oil over medium heat and stir-fry cardamom pods, cinnamon stick and cloves until fragrant, about 1 minute. Add onion and stir-fry until onion is soft, about 2 minutes. Stir in lamb, garam masala, chili powder, garlic, ginger and salt. Stir-fry until lamb changes color, 4–5 minutes. Add potatoes, tomatoes and their juice and hot water. Reduce heat to low, cover and simmer until potatoes are tender, about 8 minutes. Remove from heat and stir in cilantro and mint. Spoon into serving bowls. Serve hot with naan bread or steamed basmati rice.

Thai pork and ginger curry

Serves 4

1 stalk lemongrass, white part only, bruised and chopped

1 tablespoon peeled and grated fresh galangal

3 fresh red Thai or Anaheim chilies, coarsely chopped

1 tablespoon coriander seeds

2 teaspoons dried shrimp paste

6 cloves garlic, coarsely chopped

2 teaspoons ground turmeric

2 teaspoons Asian sesame oil

1 lb (500 g) lean pork, cut into 1-inch (2.5-cm) cubes

¼ cup peeled and finely julienned fresh ginger

1¹/₃ cups (11 fl oz/340 ml) warm water

2 tablespoons vegetable oil

1 tablespoon soy sauce

1 tablespoon packed brown sugar

2 tablespoons tamarind paste

4 scallions (shallots/spring onions), sliced

2 tablespoons fresh cilantro (fresh coriander) leaves

In a food processor, combine lemongrass, galangal, chilies, coriander seeds, shrimp paste, garlic, turmeric and sesame oil and process to a thick paste.

Put pork in a medium bowl, add paste and stir to coat evenly. Cover and refrigerate for 30 minutes.

Put ginger in a small bowl, add ¹/₃ cup (3 fl oz/90 ml) warm water and let stand for 10 minutes. Drain.

In a wok or large skillet, heat oil over medium heat and sauté pork for 10 minutes. Add remaining 1 cup (8 fl oz/ 250 ml) water, soy sauce, brown sugar and tamarind paste. Reduce heat to low and simmer until pork is tender, about 15 minutes. Add ginger and scallions. Spoon into serving bowls. Garnish with cilantro leaves and serve with steamed jasmine rice.

fish and seafood

Chili, salt and pepper squid

Serves 2–4

2 small red chilies, seeded and finely chopped

1 tablespoon sea salt

1 teaspoon cracked black pepper

2 tablespoons vegetable oil

16 baby squid (calamari), about 2 lb (1 kg), cleaned
  and halved

1½ cups (1½ oz/45 g) mizuna

In a small bowl, combine chilies, salt and pepper. Brush oil over squid pieces and press chili mixture into both sides of squid. Preheat a grill pan or barbecue. Grill squid pieces for 15–30 seconds each side. Remove from grill and serve on a bed of mizuna.

Crab chettinad

Serves 4–6

3 lb (1.5 kg) soft-shell or blue swimmer crabs

¹⁄₃ cup coriander seeds

1 cup (8 fl oz/250 ml) vegetable oil and melted
   unsalted butter combined

1-inch (2.5-cm) cinnamon stick

3 green cardamom pods

3 whole cloves

2 lb (1 kg) yellow (brown) onions, about 6 medium,
   chopped

1 teaspoon salt, plus extra salt to taste

2¹⁄₂ tablespoons grated fresh ginger

2¹⁄₂ tablespoons crushed garlic

4 teaspoons chili powder

4 teaspoons ground turmeric

2 lb (1 kg) tomatoes, about 7 medium, unpeeled,
   finely chopped

1 cup (1¹⁄₂ oz/45 g) chopped fresh cilantro (fresh
   coriander)

18 fresh curry leaves, torn into pieces

4 teaspoons crushed black peppercorns

steamed basmati rice, for serving

Remove large top shell from each crab. Remove fibrous matter from inside crab and discard. Rinse crabs well. Use a sharp knife to cut each crab in quarters. Set aside.

In a spice grinder, grind coriander seeds to a powder. Set aside.

In a large frying pan, heat oil and butter mixture over low heat. Add cinnamon, cardamom and cloves. Cook until fragrant, about 30 seconds. Add onions and 1 teaspoon salt and cook, uncovered, stirring often, until onions are dark golden brown, 15–20 minutes. Add ginger and garlic and cook for 1 minute. Add ground coriander, chili powder and turmeric, and cook, stirring, for 1 minute. Add tomatoes and cook, uncovered, stirring often, until tomatoes are cooked and soft, about 10 minutes. Add crab and cook, covered, turning pieces occasionally, until crab shells turn red and meat is just cooked, 15–20 minutes. Use tongs to remove crab pieces to a plate. Add cilantro, curry leaves and peppercorns to sauce in pan, mixing well. Taste and add salt if desired. Return crab pieces to pan and turn to coat with sauce, then serve with steamed rice.

Crab in chili oyster sauce

Serves 4–6

2 tablespoons peanut oil

2 red chilies, seeded and finely chopped

2 cloves garlic, chopped

1 tablespoon chopped fresh ginger

¼ cup (2 fl oz/60 ml) oyster sauce

½ cup (4 fl oz/125 ml) fish stock (see page 222)

2 tablespoons sweet chili sauce

2 lb (1 kg) uncooked crab, segmented

4 scallions (spring onions/shallots), chopped

In a large frying pan over medium heat, heat oil. Add chilies, garlic and ginger and sauté until fragrant, about 1 minute. Add oyster sauce, stock and sweet chili sauce and bring to boil. Simmer until slightly thickened, about 4 minutes.

Add crab segments and scallions and stir to coat with sauce. Simmer, covered, until crab is cooked through, 15–20 minutes. To test, crack a shell to see if flesh is tender.

Tips

• When eating crab meat from the shell, crack the claws with a nutcracker or meat mallet. Have lots of finger bowls and hand towels available as this can be messy.

• Serve crabs with steamed jasmine rice or Asian noodles.

Crispy fish with hot sour chili sauce

Serves 4

1 tablespoon vegetable oil

3 red chilies, seeded and chopped

2 cloves garlic, chopped

2 tablespoons chopped fresh cilantro (fresh coriander) leaves

2 tablespoons oyster sauce

1 tablespoon fish sauce

1 tablespoon sweet chili sauce

2 tablespoons lime juice

½ cup (4 fl oz/125 ml) fish stock (see page 222) or water

2 tablespoons chopped fresh basil

4 small whole fish, about 8 oz (250 g) each, scaled and cleaned

coarse salt

oil, for deep-frying

steamed jasmine rice, for serving

In a saucepan over medium heat, heat oil. Add chilies, garlic, and cilantro and cook until fragrant, about 1 minute. Pour in sauces, juice and stock and bring to a boil, stirring constantly. Cook until sauce thickens, about 4 minutes. Stir in basil.

With a sharp knife, make 2 to 3 deep diagonal cuts on each side of the fish. Rub generously with salt.

In a large saucepan over medium heat, heat oil until hot (see Tip below). Immerse fish and cook until golden and crisp, about 10 minutes. Drain on paper towels.

Serve fish with sauce and rice.

Tip

The oil must be hot enough to make the fish sizzle immediately; this will seal the surface of the fish and trap in moisture.

Fish and tomato curry

Serves 4

For spice mixture

2 tablespoons vegetable oil

1 onion, finely sliced

3 cloves garlic, finely chopped

1 teaspoon peeled and grated fresh ginger

½ teaspoon ground turmeric

1 teaspoon ground cumin

2 teaspoons ground coriander

1 teaspoon garam masala (see page 223)

½ teaspoon chili powder

1 lb (500 g) white fish fillets, cut into 2-inch (5-cm)
  pieces

13 oz (390 g) canned chopped tomatoes

1 teaspoon sea salt

1 teaspoon sugar

2 tablespoons fresh cilantro (fresh coriander) leaves

lemon wedges, for serving

To make spice mixture: In a wok or large skillet, heat oil over medium heat and stir-fry remaining ingredients until fragrant, 1–2 minutes. Add fish, tomatoes with their juice, salt and sugar. Reduce heat to low, cover and simmer, stirring occasionally, until fish is opaque throughout, 8–10 minutes. Remove from heat and spoon into serving bowls. Sprinkle with cilantro. Serve with lemon wedges and steamed basmati rice.

Fish bites with coconut sambal

Serves 4

12 oz (375 g) firm white boneless, skinless fish fillets

1½ teaspoons ground turmeric

1 teaspoon sea salt

2 teaspoons cornstarch (cornflour)

¼ teaspoon ground chili powder

2 tablespoons vegetable oil

2 cups (10 oz/300 g) steamed jasmine rice

2 tablespoons chopped fresh cilantro (fresh
  coriander) leaves

garlic chives, for garnish

For coconut sambal

⅓ cup (1½ oz/45 g) unsweetened dried
  (desiccated) shredded coconut

3 tablespoons boiling water

½ teaspoon shrimp paste

1 fresh kaffir lime leaf, finely shredded

¼ onion, finely chopped

2 teaspoons lemon juice

Cut fish into ¾-inch by 2½-inch (2-cm by 6-cm) lengths. In a bowl, combine turmeric, salt, cornstarch and chili powder and mix well. Rub spice mixture into fish pieces. Preheat a grill pan or barbecue, then brush grill with oil. Grill fish pieces until fish is firm, 1–2 minutes each side. Remove from grill. Combine cooked rice with cilantro. Serve fish bites with rice and coconut sambal. Garnish with garlic chives.

To make coconut sambal: Place coconut in a heatproof bowl, pour in boiling water and mix well. Add shrimp paste, kaffir lime leaf, onion and lemon juice. Cover and refrigerate until serving.

Fish in coconut sauce

Serves 4

1 lb (500 g) white-fleshed fish fillets, such as snapper,
  barramundi or ocean perch

3 tablespoons vegetable oil

1 teaspoon brown or black mustard seeds

1/2 teaspoon fenugreek seeds

3 dried red chilies

1 lb (500 g) yellow (brown) onions, about 3 medium,
  halved and thinly sliced

2 tablespoons grated fresh ginger

2 tablespoons crushed garlic

36 fresh curry leaves

3 teaspoons ground turmeric

2–4 tablespoons chili powder

2 tomatoes, unpeeled, coarsely chopped

1 1/2 cups (12 fl oz/375 ml) coconut cream

1 teaspoon tamarind concentrate

salt to taste

juice of 1/2 lemon

steamed basmati rice

Remove skin from fish fillets then cut fish into ³/₄-inch x
2-inch (2-cm x 5-cm) pieces. Set aside.

In a karhai or wok, heat oil over low heat. Add mustard
seeds and cook until seeds crackle, about 30 seconds.
Add fenugreek seeds and chilies, and cook, stirring, until
seeds turn light golden brown and chilies are deep golden
brown, about 30 seconds. Add onions and cook, stirring,
until slightly softened, about 1 minute. Add ginger and
garlic and cook, stirring, for 1 minute. Add curry leaves,
turmeric and chili powder and cook, stirring, for
30 seconds. Add tomatoes and cook until tomatoes are
slightly soft, about 3 minutes. Stir in coconut cream and
tamarind and season with salt.

Stir in fish pieces and simmer, covered, until fish is just
cooked through, about 5 minutes. Stir in lemon juice.
Serve immediately with rice.

Fish steamed in banana leaves

Serves 6

peeled flesh from 1 fresh coconut (about 12 oz/375 g), coarsely chopped

6 fresh green chilies, coarsely chopped

$^2/_3$ cup (1 oz/30 g) chopped fresh cilantro (fresh coriander)

$^1/_2$ cup ($^3/_4$ oz/20 g) chopped fresh mint

$^1/_4$ cup (2 fl oz/60 ml) vegetable oil

2 teaspoons crushed garlic

$^1/_2$ teaspoon ground turmeric

1 teaspoon cumin seeds

juice of 2 limes

$^1/_4$ teaspoon sugar

salt to taste

5 fresh banana leaves, center veins removed

2 lb (1 kg) large, white-fleshed fish fillets such as barramundi, ocean perch or snapper, cut into 10 serving-sized portions

lime wedges, for serving

In a food processor, combine coconut, chilies, cilantro, mint, oil, garlic, turmeric, cumin seeds, lime juice, sugar and salt. Process until finely minced to make a coconut chutney. Divide evenly into 10 portions and set aside.

Slowly pass each banana leaf over a medium–high gas flame until leaf turns bright green. Alternatively, heat a heavy frying pan over medium–high heat, place leaf in pan and heat until leaf turns bright green. Let leaves cool and cut into pieces large enough to wrap a fish portion each.

Place a fish piece on a banana leaf piece. Spread a portion of coconut chutney over the fish. Wrap leaf around fish and tie with kitchen twine to secure. Repeat with remaining fish pieces, banana leaves and coconut chutney.

Place fish parcels in a large bamboo steamer over a large wok half-filled with boiling water. Steam until fish flakes when tested with a fork, 12–15 minutes. Serve hot with lime wedges.

Tips

Heating banana leaves makes them malleable and easy to fold. If banana leaves are unavailable, use parchment (baking) paper or aluminum foil.

Fried fish with chili sauce

Serves 6

4 dried chilies

¼ cup (2 fl oz/60 ml) boiling water

1 tablespoon vegetable oil

2 cloves garlic, finely chopped

2 tablespoons Chinese chili sauce

4 tablespoons tomato ketchup

1 cup (8 fl oz/250 ml) chicken stock (see page 218)

1 teaspoon superfine (caster) sugar

2 teaspoons cornstarch (cornflour) mixed with
   1 tablespoon water

sea salt to taste

3 scallions (shallots/spring onions), white parts only

1 tablespoon cornstarch (cornflour)

3 eggs, beaten

6 firm white-fleshed fish fillets, cut into 3-inch
   (7.5-cm) pieces

3 cups (24 fl oz/750 ml) vegetable oil for deep-frying

Place chilies in a small bowl, add boiling water and soak for 30 minutes. Drain and finely chop.

In a small saucepan over medium heat, warm oil. Add garlic and cook until aromatic, about 1 minute. Add chili sauce, ketchup, stock, sugar and chilies. Bring to a boil, reduce heat to simmer and cook for 3 minutes. Add cornstarch-water mixture and stir until sauce thickens slightly, about 3 minutes. Season with salt and set chili sauce aside.

Cut scallions into 2½-inch (6-cm) lengths. Slice each piece lengthwise into fine strips. Place in a bowl of ice water and refrigerate until scallions curl, about 15 minutes. Drain.

Preheat oven to 225°F (110°C/Gas ¼).

In a small bowl, whisk cornstarch and eggs together. Add fish pieces and stir gently until coated in batter. In a wok or saucepan, heat oil until it reaches 375°F (190°C) on a deep-frying thermometer or until a small bread cube dropped in oil sizzles and turns golden. Working in

batches, lift fish, one piece at a time, from batter, allowing excess batter to drain off, and carefully place in hot oil. Cook until golden, turning once, 3–4 minutes total. Using a slotted spoon, remove fish from hot oil and drain on paper towels. Place on a heatproof dish and keep warm in preheated oven. Repeat with remaining fish. Place fish on individual plates, drizzle with chili sauce and top with scallion curls. Serve remaining chili sauce in a separate bowl.

Fried octopus with chili sauce and noodles

Serves 4

6½ oz (200 g) octopus or squid (calamari), cleaned
   and rubbed with salt
3 oz (90 g) fresh button mushrooms
6 medium scallions (shallots/spring onions)
3 fresh red chilies
1 small yellow (brown) onion
1 tablespoon vegetable or sunflower oil, for frying
5 oz (150 g) somyeon noodles (wheat-flour noodles)

For sauce
2 tablespoons red chili paste
2 tablespoons red chili powder
2 teaspoons light soy sauce
1 tablespoon crushed garlic
1 tablespoon finely chopped scallion (shallot/spring
   onion)
1 teaspoon sugar
pinch of freshly ground black pepper
2 tablespoons Asian sesame oil
1 tablespoon pan-toasted, ground sesame seeds
1 tablespoon vegetable or sunflower oil

Wash octopus to remove the salt. Cut body and tentacles into 2½-inch (6-cm) long pieces. Bring a medium-sized saucepan of salted water to a boil. Immerse octopus pieces in boiling water and remove just as it starts to curl, 2–3 minutes.

Bring a small saucepan of water to a boil. Cut mushrooms in half, then dip in boiling water for a few seconds. Remove and drain.

Cut scallions into 1½-inch (4-cm) lengths. Slice chilies lengthwise. Remove core and seeds and cut flesh into thin strips about 1½ inches (4 cm) long. Peel onion and cut into bite-sized pieces.

In a medium-sized bowl, combine sauce ingredients and mix well.

In a frying pan, heat 1 tablespoon oil and stir-fry vegetables for about 2 minutes. Add octopus and sauce. Continue to stir-fry for 2–3 minutes, then remove from heat and cover to keep warm.

Meanwhile, bring 4 cups (32 fl oz/1 L) water to a boil. Add noodles and boil for 3 minutes. Remove from water, rinse thoroughly in cold water and drain.

Serve hot octopus and cold noodles on a large plate.

Garlic and chili scallops

Serves 2–3

1 lb (500 g) scallops

3 cloves garlic, finely chopped

$\frac{1}{2}$ teaspoon five spice powder

1 teaspoon grated fresh ginger

1 small red chili, seeded and finely chopped

2 tablespoons soy sauce

1 tablespoon rice wine

2 tablespoons vegetable oil

3 tablespoons water

1 cup (1 oz/30 g) mizuna

Place scallops in a shallow nonmetallic dish. In a bowl, combine garlic, five spice powder, ginger, chili, soy sauce and rice wine and pour over scallops. Cover dish with plastic wrap and refrigerate for 30 minutes. Drain scallops, reserving marinade. Preheat a grill pan or barbecue, then brush grill with oil. Grill scallops until the opaque flesh turns white, 2–3 minutes, turning during cooking. Remove from grill.

Place reserved marinade into a saucepan. Add water, bring to a boil and allow to boil for 1 minute; set aside. To serve, arrange mizuna on serving plates. Top with scallops and drizzle with warm marinade.

Goan fish

Serves 4–6

1–1½ cups dried red chilies broken into small
pieces
⅓ cup coriander seeds
¼ cup cumin seeds
¾ cup (6 fl oz/180 ml) white vinegar
1 tablespoon finely grated fresh ginger
1 tablespoon crushed garlic
2 teaspoons ground turmeric
½ cup (4 fl oz/125 ml) vegetable oil and melted
   unsalted butter combined
1 lb (500 g) yellow (brown) onions, about 3 medium,
   halved and sliced
2 large tomatoes, unpeeled, quartered
2 fresh green chilies, slit lengthwise
2½ cups (20 fl oz/625 ml) coconut milk
salt to taste
2 lb (1 kg) white-fleshed fish fillets such as snapper,
   ling, cod or ocean perch
steamed basmati rice

In a spice grinder, grind dried chilis, coriander seeds and
cumin seeds to a powder. Place in a bowl and combine
with vinegar, ginger, garlic and turmeric to form a paste.
Set aside.

In a large karhai or wok, heat oil and butter mixture over
medium–low heat. Add onions and cook, uncovered,
stirring often, until soft, about 10 minutes. Add spice paste
and cook, stirring, until fragrant, about 3 minutes. Add
tomatoes, green chilies and coconut milk and cook,
uncovered, stirring often, until tomatoes soften, about
5 minutes. Season with salt.

If fish fillets are large, cut into serving-sized pieces. Add
fish to sauce and cook, uncovered, until fish flakes when
tested with a fork, about 5 minutes. Serve hot with
steamed rice.

Green fish and oven-roasted potato curry

Serves 4

4 potatoes, peeled

3 tablespoons vegetable oil

2 tablespoons green curry paste (see page 227)

2 cups (16 fl oz/500 ml) coconut milk

6 fresh kaffir lime leaves

1 tablespoon fish sauce

1 lb (500 g) swordfish fillets, cut into 1½-inch (4-cm) chunks

2 tablespoons chopped fresh basil leaves

2 tablespoons chopped fresh cilantro (fresh coriander)

Preheat oven to 400°F (200°C/Gas 6). Cut each potato into 6 chunks. Put potatoes in an oiled roasting pan and coat with 2 tablespoons oil. Bake until golden and crisp, about 15 minutes.

Meanwhile, in a wok or large skillet, heat remaining 1 tablespoon oil over medium heat. Add curry paste and fry until fragrant, about 30 seconds. Add coconut milk, lime leaves, fish sauce and fish. Reduce heat to low and simmer until fish is opaque throughout, 10–12 minutes. Remove from heat and stir in basil, cilantro and baked potatoes. Spoon into serving bowls. Serve with steamed jasmine rice.

Grilled lobster tails with rougail sauce

Serves 6

1/2-inch (1.2-cm) piece fresh turmeric, peeled, or
  2 teaspoons ground turmeric
5 garlic cloves, crushed in a garlic press
2 tablespoons finely chopped brown or pink
  shallots (French shallots)
1 fresh long red chili, seeded and finely chopped
2 stalks lemongrass, white part only, peeled and
  finely chopped
2 tablespoons fish sauce
juice of 1 lime
3 tablespoons vegetable or olive oil
1 teaspoon ground pepper
3 rock lobster tails, halved lengthwise, about 6 oz
  (180 g) each
nuoc cham nem sauce (see page 225) or fish sauce
1–2 lemons or limes, quartered or cut into wedges

1 fresh long red or green chili, seeded and thinly
  sliced
fresh cilantro (fresh coriander) sprigs, for garnish

If using fresh turmeric, pound in a mortar using a pestle or alternatively use a grater. Soak extracted juice and pulp in 1 tablespoon water, from 3–4 minutes up to a few hours; then strain. Wear gloves to prevent turmeric staining your skin. In a large nonmetallic bowl, combine turmeric mixture or ground turmeric and garlic, shallots, chili, lemongrass, fish sauce, lime juice, oil and pepper.

Rinse lobster halves and pat dry. Place in sauce and let stand for 1 hour, turning occasionally to coat all sides.

Prepare a charcoal grill (barbecue) or brazier or preheat an oven broiler (grill). Cook lobster, turning once and spooning additional marinade atop occasionally during cooking, until opaque throughout, about 10 minutes without shell and about 12 minutes with shell. If broiling (grilling), cook lobster, flesh-side up, about 4 inches (10 cm) from heat source, for 10–15 minutes.

Place lobster on serving plate. Serve hot with nuoc cham nem sauce or simple fish sauce, lemon or lime wedges, chili slices and cilantro sprigs.

Tips

• Rougail is a generic French term applied to any number of spicy sauces, especially those served in tropical countries.

• Instead of chopping all the sauce ingredient separately, combine them in a food processor, and puree.

Indian cuttlefish casserole

Serves 4

2 tablespoons vegetable oil

1 onion, sliced

2 cloves garlic, chopped

2 red chilies, seeded and chopped

2 teaspoons ground cumin

1 teaspoon ground coriander

1 teaspoon ground fenugreek seed

1/2 teaspoon chili powder

1 cup (8 fl oz/250 ml) fish stock (see page 222)

2 lb (1 kg) cuttlefish, cleaned and scored (see Tips below)

cooked rice or noodles, for serving

In a saucepan over medium heat, heat oil. Add onion and cook until tender, about 4 minutes. Add garlic, chilies, cumin, coriander, fenugreek and chili powder and cook 1 minute. Stir in stock and bring to a boil.

Add cuttlefish and simmer, uncovered, until tender, about 5 minutes. Serve with rice or noodles.

Tips

• To prepare cuttlefish, place on work surface bone-side down and cut down the length of the body, but do not pierce intestines and ink sac. Open body and discard gut, head and tentacles. Firmly pull skin off two remaining fleshy pieces. Score flesh with diamond-grid cuts.

• Other types of seafood can be used instead, including 1 1/2 lb (750 g) uncooked shrimp (prawns) or 2 lb (1 kg) octopus, which will need simmering for 30 minutes.

Indian shrimp curry

Serves 4

1 tablespoon vegetable oil

1 teaspoon chili powder

1 tablespoon ground sweet paprika

1/2 teaspoon ground turmeric

3 cloves garlic, finely chopped

2 teaspoons peeled and grated fresh ginger

1 tablespoon ground coriander

1 teaspoon ground cumin

2 teaspoons packed brown sugar

1 1/4 cups (10 fl oz/300 ml) water

1 3/4 cups (14 fl oz/440 ml) coconut milk

1 teaspoon sea salt

2 tablespoons tamarind paste

1 1/2 lb (750 g) jumbo shrimp (king prawns), shelled and deveined, tails intact

In a wok or large skillet, heat oil over medium heat and stir-fry chili powder, paprika, turmeric, garlic, ginger, coriander and cumin until fragrant, about 30 seconds. Stir in brown sugar and water. Bring to a boil, reduce heat to low and simmer for 5 minutes. Add coconut milk, salt, tamarind paste and shrimp. Stir over medium heat until shrimp turn pink, 4–5 minutes. Remove from heat. Spoon into serving dishes. Serve with steamed basmati rice.

Lime and chili sardines with green aioli

Serves 4

36 fresh sardines, cleaned, heads removed and
   butterflied

2 tablespoons vegetable oil

1 teaspoon grated lime zest (rind)

1 tablespoon lime juice

1 small red chili, seeded and finely chopped

1 tablespoon chopped fresh cilantro (coriander) leaves

1/4 teaspoon sea salt

1/4 teaspoon freshly ground black pepper

11/2 cups (11/2 oz/45 g) mizuna

For green aioli

6 scallions (shallots/spring onions), coarsely chopped

1/4 cup (1/3 oz/10 g) chopped fresh basil leaves

3 cloves garlic, chopped

3 egg yolks

2 tablespoons lemon juice

3/4 cup (6 fl oz/180 ml) virgin olive oil

sea salt and freshly ground black pepper

Pat sardines dry with paper towel and place in a shallow nonmetallic dish. In a small bowl, combine 2 tablespoons oil, zest, juice, chili, cilantro, salt and pepper and mix well. Brush over sardines and let stand for 5 minutes. Preheat a grill pan or barbecue, then brush grill with oil. Grill sardines for 1–2 minutes each side. Remove from grill. To serve, arrange mizuna on serving plates and top with warm sardines. Serve with green aioli.

To make green aioli: In a food processor, combine scallions, basil, garlic, egg yolks and lemon juice. Process until smooth, about 30 seconds. Gradually add olive oil while food processor motor is running and process until the mixture becomes a thick sauce. Add salt and pepper to taste.

Mussel curry

Serves 4

1 tablespoon vegetable oil

1 onion, finely chopped

6 cloves garlic, finely chopped

2 fresh green Thai or Anaheim chilies, seeded and chopped

1 teaspoon ground turmeric

½ cup (4 fl oz/125 ml) white wine vinegar

1¾ cups (14 fl oz/440 ml) coconut milk

2 teaspoons sugar

2 lb (1 kg) mussels, scrubbed and debearded

2 tablespoons chopped fresh cilantro (fresh coriander)

sea salt to taste

In a large saucepan, heat oil over medium heat and fry onion, garlic, chilies and turmeric until fragrant, 2–3 minutes. Add vinegar, coconut milk, sugar and mussels. Bring to a boil, reduce heat to low, cover, and simmer until mussels have opened, about 6 minutes. Remove from heat and discard any mussels that have not opened. Stir in cilantro and salt. Transfer mussels to serving bowls. Pour sauce over and serve with steamed rice.

Red curry shrimp

Serves 4

2 cups (14 oz/440 g) jasmine rice

3 cups (24 fl oz/750 ml) boiling water (from a kettle)

2 cups (16 fl oz/500 ml) coconut milk

2 tablespoons red curry paste (see page 227)

2 tablespoons fish sauce

1 long red chili, halved and seeded

1½ lb (750 g) jumbo shrimp (green king prawns),
peeled and deveined, tails intact

2 fresh kaffir lime leaves, finely shredded or
½ teaspoon grated lime zest (rind), for garnish

Place rice in a fine-mesh sieve and rinse with cold running water until water is clear. Drain and place in a saucepan with boiling water. Cover and bring to a boil over high heat. Reduce heat to low and cook for about 15 minutes. Remove from heat and stand for 5 minutes. Fluff with a fork.

In a saucepan over low heat, combine coconut milk, curry paste, fish sauce and chili. Stir until heated through, about 5 minutes; do not boil. Add shrimp and cook, stirring, until shrimp change color, about 15 minutes. Serve hot with jasmine rice. Garnish with shredded lime leaves.

Let coconut milk stand until the thick coconut milk rises to the top. Spoon the thick coconut milk into a bowl, reserving 2 tablespoons for garnish. Heat oil in a wok or large frying pan over medium-high heat and fry the curry paste, stirring constantly, until fragrant, 1–2 minutes. Add the thick coconut milk, stir to combine, and bring to a boil. Add eggplant, bamboo shoots and remaining thin coconut milk. Reduce heat and simmer, uncovered, until vegetables are slightly soft, about 4 minutes.

Tear 2 kaffir lime leaves and basil into pieces. Stir fish sauce, lime leaves and chilies into curry. Add fish and cook until fish flakes when tested with a fork, about 2 minutes. Add half the basil leaves and remove from heat.

Transfer curry to a serving dish and garnish with remaining basil. Drizzle with 2 tablespoons reserved thick coconut milk. Roll remaining lime leaf into a tight cylinder and cut into fine strips; sprinkle over curry.

Tips

Most varieties of fish fillet will suit here, but don't stir too vigorously or the pieces may break up. Firm-textured fish, such as cod or even sturgeon, hold up best but may require longer cooking time.

Red curry with fish

Serves 4–6

about 2 cups (16 fl oz/500 ml) coconut milk
2–3 tablespoons vegetable oil
1/4 cup (2 fl oz/60 ml) red curry paste (see page 227)
1/2 cup (2 oz/60 g) chopped round Thai or purple
  eggplant (aubergine)
1 cup (3 1/2 oz/100 g) coarsely chopped fresh or
  canned bamboo shoots, rinsed and drained
3 kaffir lime leaves, stemmed
1 cup (1 oz/30 g) loosely packed, fresh sweet Thai
  basil leaves
1–2 tablespoons fish sauce, to taste
12 oz (375 g) fish fillets such as snapper, bream, or
  perch, thinly sliced
2 fresh long red chilies, cut into large pieces

Salmon with sweet pepper sauce

Serves 4

3 tablespoons vegetable oil

1 small red chili, seeded and chopped

2 cloves garlic, crushed

1 red bell pepper (capsicum), seeded and diced

2 tablespoons palm sugar or brown sugar

1 tablespoon rice vinegar

1 tablespoon soy sauce

1 cup (8 fl oz/250 ml) water

2 teaspoons cornstarch (cornflour) combined with
    1 tablespoon water

2 teaspoons lemon juice

6½ oz (180 g) egg noodles

3 teaspoons Asian sesame oil

1 tablespoon lime juice

2 tablespoons chopped fresh cilantro (fresh
    coriander)

4 salmon fillets, about 6½ oz (200 g) each

In a wok or frying pan over medium–high heat, warm 1 tablespoon vegetable oil. Add chili, garlic and bell pepper and cook, stirring occasionally, until bell pepper is softened, about 3 minutes. Stir in sugar, vinegar, soy sauce and water. Reduce heat to low and simmer until flavors are blended, about 5 minutes. Stir in cornstarch and water. Continuing to stir, bring sauce to a boil and cook until thickened, 2–3 minutes. Remove from heat and stir in lemon juice.

Cook noodles as directed on package or on page 23. Drain. In a small bowl, combine sesame oil, lime juice and cilantro. Mix well. Pour over noodles and toss to coat.

In a frying pan over medium–high heat, warm remaining 2 tablespoons vegetable oil. Add salmon fillets and cook until fish flakes easily when tested with a fork, 2–3 minutes on each side.

To serve, reheat sweet pepper sauce if necessary. Arrange noodles and salmon fillets on individual plates. Spoon sauce on top and serve immediately.

Seafood hot pot

Serves 4

8 cups (64 fl oz/2 L) fish stock (see page 222)
2-inch (5-cm) piece fresh ginger, peeled
1 teaspoon chili paste
2 tablespoons Asian sesame oil
2 lb (1 kg) jumbo shrimp (king prawns), peeled and
    deveined, tails intact
8 oz (250 g) firm white-fleshed fish fillets, cut into bite-
    size pieces
8 oz (250 g) squid (calamari) rings
6½ oz (200 g) scallops, cleaned
2 small bok choy, leaves separated and trimmed
4 oz (125 g) snow peas (mange-tout), trimmed
6½ oz (200 g) egg noodles

Place stock in saucepan. Bring to a boil, reduce heat to
low and simmer for 5 minutes. Add ginger, chili paste and
sesame oil and simmer until flavors are blended, about
5 minutes. Transfer stock to hot pot. Arrange seafood and
vegetables on a platter, and place platter and hot pot on
table.

Using chopsticks, guests dip seafood and vegetables into
hot stock and cook until tender, 1–2 minutes.

After seafood and vegetables are cooked, add noodles to
stock and cook until tender, about 3 minutes. Stock and
noodles are then ladled into individual bowls and served.

Tip
A hot pot keeps the aromatic stock hot at the table. A
fondue set or an electric frying pan can also be used if a
traditional hot pot is unavailable.

Shrimp korma

Serves 4

1 onion, chopped

2 teaspoons chopped fresh ginger

2 red chilies, seeded and chopped

2 cloves garlic, chopped

1/3 cup (2 oz/60 g) chopped cashews

2 teaspoons ground coriander

2 teaspoons ground cumin

1 teaspoon garam masala (see page 223)

1/4 teaspoon cinnamon

1/4 teaspoon ground cardamom

1/2 cup (4 fl oz/125 ml) water

2 tablespoons olive oil

7 oz (220 g) plain (natural) whole-milk yogurt

salt

1 1/2 lb (750 g) uncooked shrimp (prawns), peeled and
  deveined

3 tablespoons chopped fresh cilantro (fresh coriander)
  leaves

steamed rice, for serving

In a food processor, combine onion, ginger, chilies, garlic
and cashews and grind finely. Add coriander, cumin,
garam masala, cinnamon, cardamom, and water and
process.

In a large saucepan over medium heat, heat oil. Add
processed mixture and cook until fragrant, about
1–2 minutes. Add yogurt and salt to taste and bring to
boil. Simmer 5 minutes, stirring occasionally. Add shrimp
and cook until tender, 3–5 minutes. Stir in cilantro and
serve with rice.

Sizzling teriyaki and ginger fish in banana leaves

Serves 4

4 whole snappers, 8–12 oz (250–375 g) each

2 tablespoons Asian sesame oil

2 stalks lemongrass, white part only, trimmed

1 bunch fresh cilantro (fresh coriander), stemmed

¼ cup peeled and finely julienned fresh ginger

8 scallions (shallots/spring onions), cut into ¾-inch
  (2-cm) diagonal slices

1 small red bell pepper (capsicum), seeded and
  thinly sliced

2 banana leaves, softened and halved

¾ cup (6 fl oz/180 ml) peanut oil

¼ cup (2 fl oz/60 ml) Japanese teriyaki sauce

chopped fresh cilantro (fresh coriander), for garnish

Rub fish inside and out with sesame oil. Make 2 or 3 diagonal cuts through thickest part of flesh on each side of fish. Cut lemongrass to fit inside fish and bruise lemongrass by hitting with knife or meat mallet. Place one half of each lemongrass stalk inside fish, along with one-fourth cilantro. Scatter ginger, scallions and pepper over each fish, and wrap in softened banana leaf. Place 2 fish in each level of a 12-inch (30-cm) bamboo steamer or steamer basket and cover.

To soften banana leaves: Remove hard stems and drop banana leaves into hot water for 30–60 seconds. Drain and pat dry with paper towels.

Partially fill wok or pot with water (steamer should not touch water) and bring to a rapid simmer. Place two-level steamer over boiling water and steam, until fish flakes when tested with a fork and is opaque, 15–20 minutes, depending on size. Switch level of steamer halfway through for even cooking.

Lift fish parcels out of steamer and place on serving plates. In a small saucepan, heat peanut oil until it smokes, and immediately pour over each fish. This will make a great sizzling sound. Drizzle teriyaki sauce over fish and garnish with chopped cilantro.

Spicy tomato and leek shrimp with Hokkien noodles

Serves 4–6

2 lb (1 kg) uncooked jumbo shrimp (prawns), shelled
and deveined

1 tablespoon olive oil

2 cloves garlic, crushed

1 leek, white part only, sliced and washed

1 small green bell pepper (capsicum), seeded and
diced

2 tablespoons tomato paste

3 large tomatoes (1 lb/500 g), skinned and chopped

2 teaspoons balsamic vinegar

1 tablespoon chopped fresh basil

1 tablespoon chopped fresh oregano

½ cup (4 fl oz/125 ml) dry white wine

1 lb (500 g) Hokkien noodles (wheat noodles)

Put shrimp in a large bamboo steamer or steamer basket, and cover. In a large saucepan slightly larger in diameter than steamer, heat olive oil and sauté garlic and leek for 2–3 minutes, without browning. Add pepper and tomato paste and cook until paste starts to darken and becomes aromatic, 2–3 minutes. Add tomatoes, vinegar, basil, oregano and wine. Place steamer over pan and steam until shrimp turn pink, 3–6 minutes depending on size. (Remove shrimp from heat and continue to simmer sauce if thicker sauce is preferred.)

Cover noodles with hot water for 1–2 minutes. Drain, separate with a fork and place in a large bowl. Stir in sauce and shrimp.

Spicy tomato octopus

Serves 4

2 tablespoons butter

1 onion, chopped

2 cloves garlic, chopped

2 teaspoons ground cumin

2 teaspoons ground coriander

1 teaspoon turmeric

¼ teaspoon chili powder

14 oz (440 g) canned peeled tomatoes, chopped

salt and freshly ground pepper

2 lb (1 kg) octopus, cleaned and segmented

½ cup (4 fl oz/125 ml) light whipping cream

steamed rice, for serving

In a saucepan over medium heat, heat butter. Add onion and cook until tender, about 5 minutes. Stir in garlic, cumin, coriander, turmeric and chili powder and cook 1 minute. Pour in tomatoes, cover and simmer 15 minutes, stirring occasionally.

Season with salt and pepper. Add octopus and simmer until tender, about 40–50 minutes. Stir in cream and heat through. Serve with rice.

Sri Lankan seafood curry

Serves 4

2 tablespoons vegetable oil

1 teaspoon ground coriander

1 teaspoon ground cumin

1 teaspoon fennel seeds

½ teaspoon ground cinnamon

1 teaspoon yellow mustard seeds

½ teaspoon chili flakes

½ teaspoon ground cloves

1 teaspoon ground cardamom

1 lb (500 g) swordfish fillets, cut into 2-inch (5-cm) chunks

2 extra tablespoons vegetable oil

1 onion, chopped

4 cloves garlic, finely chopped

1 stalk lemongrass, white part only, bruised

2 teaspoons peeled and grated fresh ginger

2 teaspoons ground turmeric

8 fresh curry leaves

14 oz (440 g) canned chopped tomatoes

⅔ cup (5 fl oz/160 ml) fish stock (see page 222)

12 jumbo shrimp (king prawns), shelled and deveined, tails intact

5½ oz (170 g) fresh or lump crabmeat, picked over for shell

salt to taste

To make spice mixture: In a skillet, heat oil over medium heat. Add coriander, cumin, fennel, cinnamon, mustard seeds, chili flakes, cloves and cardamom and cook, stirring, until fragrant, about 1 minute. Remove from heat and let cool. Put fish in a baking dish. Brush with spice mixture and toss to coat. Cover and refrigerate for 30 minutes.

In a wok or large skillet, heat 1 tablespoon oil over medium heat and fry onion and garlic until onion is soft, about 1 minute. Stir in lemongrass, ginger, turmeric, and curry leaves and fry for 1 minute. Add tomatoes with their juice, and broth, reduce heat to low and simmer for 5 minutes.

In a large skillet, heat remaining 1 tablespoon oil over medium heat and fry fish until lightly browned on each side, 2–3 minutes. Add tomato mixture, shrimp and crabmeat. Cover and simmer, stirring occasionally, until shrimp are pink, about 5 minutes. Add salt. Spoon into serving bowls. Serve with steamed basmati rice.

Steamed lemon-pepper fish

Serves 2

1 whole snapper, about 1 lb (500 g)

4 fresh kaffir lime leaves or 1 teaspoon grated lime zest (rind)

2 teaspoons fish sauce

2 teaspoons oyster sauce

1 tablespoon fresh lime juice

1 teaspoon Asian sesame oil

2 teaspoons peeled and grated ginger

1 lemongrass stalk, trimmed and finely sliced

8 garlic chives, finely chopped

1/2 teaspoon ground or whole roasted Szechwan peppercorns

lime halves, for serving

Using a sharp knife, make 3 deep slits in each side of fish. Place lime leaves in fish cavity. In a small bowl, combine fish sauce, oyster sauce, lime juice, sesame oil and ginger and brush over fish. Place fish on a lightly oiled heatproof plate that will fit inside a bamboo steamer. Sprinkle with lemongrass, garlic chives and pepper.

Half fill a large wok with water (steamer should not touch water) and bring to a boil. Place fish in steamer. Cover, place steamer over boiling water and cook until fish is done, about 20 minutes, adding more water to wok when necessary. Lift steamer from wok and carefully remove fish from steamer. Serve warm, drizzled with cooking juices and accompanied with lime halves.

Steamed whole fish with miso-tamarind sauce

Serves 4

2-inch (5-cm) piece tamarind pulp

½ cup (4 fl oz/125 ml) hot water

2–3 tablespoons red miso

2 tablespoons palm or brown sugar

2 tablespoons shaoxing wine

2 cloves garlic, finely chopped

1 teaspoon grated fresh ginger

1 stalk lemongrass, white part only, peeled

2 whole snappers (about 1½ lb/750 g each), cleaned

2 scallions (shallots/spring onions), cut into
   1-inch (2.5-cm) diagonal slices

2 medium red chilies, seeded and sliced

2 tablespoons chopped fresh cilantro (fresh
   coriander) leaves (optional)

In a small bowl, combine tamarind and hot water and let stand for 10 minutes. Strain, pressing on solids with back of a spoon. Combine tamarind juice with miso, sugar, wine, garlic and ginger, stirring until smooth. Set aside.

Cut lemongrass into 4-inch (10-cm) lengths. Cut these in half lengthwise and put pieces inside fish. Make 3 diagonal cuts on each side of fish. Lay each fish on a square of parchment (baking) paper. Cover each side of fish with one-half of miso mixture and scatter one-half of scallions and chilies over. Fold top and bottom of paper, twisting ends and tucking them under to secure. Refrigerate for 1–2 hours to marinate, turning occasionally.

Cook in a covered steamer over rapidly simmering water until opaque throughout, about 15 minutes. Spoon juices over fish and sprinkle with cilantro to serve.

Thai grilled seafood curry

Serves 4

12 jumbo shrimp (king prawns), peeled and
  deveined, leaving tails intact

16 scallops, cleaned

12 oz (375 g) swordfish, cut into 2½-inch (6-cm)
  chunks

¼ cup (2 fl oz/60 ml) peanut oil

6½ oz (200 g) baby green beans

3–4 teaspoons ready-made green curry paste, to
  taste (see page 227)

2 teaspoons additional peanut oil

2 cloves garlic, finely chopped

1½ cups (12 fl oz/375 ml) thin coconut cream or
  coconut milk

3 kaffir lime leaves, crushed

3 teaspoons fish sauce

2 teaspoons soy sauce

1 teaspoon shaved palm sugar or brown sugar

1 tablespoon chopped fresh basil leaves

1 tablespoon chopped fresh cilantro (fresh coriander)
  leaves

Pat seafood dry with paper towel and brush with oil. Preheat a grill pan or barbecue. Working in batches, grill shrimp until shrimp change color, 2–3 minutes, then remove from heat. Grill scallops until the opaque flesh turns white, 2–3 minutes, then remove from heat. Grill fish pieces until flesh is firm, 2–3 minutes, then remove from heat.

Blanch green beans in a saucepan of boiling water for 2 minutes, then drain. Combine beans and seafood, cover and keep warm.

In a wok or saucepan over medium heat, combine curry paste, 2 teaspoons oil and garlic. Stir until aromatic, about 2 minutes. Stir in thin coconut cream, lime leaves, fish sauce, soy sauce and sugar. Reduce heat to low and simmer for 10 minutes. Do not allow to boil. Remove from heat and stir in basil and cilantro. Divide seafood and beans among serving bowls and spoon curry sauce over each bowl. Serve with steamed jasmine rice.

vegetables and salads

Asian coconut and crisp vegetable salad

Serves 4

1 cup (8 fl oz/250 ml) water

1/2 cup (2 oz/60 g) unsweetened dried (desiccated) shredded coconut

1 teaspoon shrimp paste

1 teaspoon chili powder or to taste

1 clove garlic, finely chopped

1/2 teaspoon brown sugar

2 tablespoons fresh lime juice

2 cups (21/2 oz/75 g) watercress

1 carrot, peeled and julienned

8 small red radishes, trimmed and julienned

1/2 English (hothouse) cucumber, peeled, seeded and thinly sliced

1 cup (4 oz/125 g) bean sprouts

4 scallions (shallots/spring onions), sliced

2 fresh kaffir lime leaves, finely shredded, or 1/2 teaspoon grated lime zest (rind)

In a small saucepan over medium heat, combine water, coconut, shrimp paste, chili powder, garlic and sugar. Stir until mixture boils and cook for 3 minutes. Remove from heat and allow to cool completely. Stir in lime juice. Chill coconut mixture until ready to serve.

In a large bowl, combine watercress, carrot, radishes, cucumber, bean sprouts, scallions and lime leaves. Toss until well combined. Add coconut mixture and toss again. Serve immediately.

Aviyal curry

Serves 4–6

8 oz (250 g) unsweetened dried (desiccated) shredded
   coconut
1¼ cups (1/2 pint/300 ml) water
¼ cup (2 oz/50 g) butter or margarine
1 oz (25 g) fresh ginger, peeled and finely chopped
3 cloves garlic, crushed
2 onions, peeled and chopped
2 teaspoons ground coriander
1 tablespoon garam masala (see page 223)
1 teaspoon turmeric
1 teaspoon salt
8 oz (250 g) broccoli, cut into small florets
2 green bell peppers (capsicums), seeded and sliced
8 oz (250 g) carrots, peeled and sliced
4–6 oz (125–185 g) green beans, trimmed and halved
   or quartered
1 green chili, seeded and finely chopped
chopped fresh cilantro (fresh coriander) or parsley, for
   garnish

In a food processor or blender, puree coconut and water until smooth.

In a heavy-based pan, heat the butter. Add ginger and garlic and fry for a few minutes. Add onions and cook until golden brown, stirring occasionally. Add coriander, garam masala, turmeric and salt and simmer for 2–3 minutes. Add vegetables and chili and continue to cook gently for 3–4 minutes, stirring well occasionally. Add coconut puree and bring mixture to a boil. Cover and simmer for about 10 minutes. Adjust seasonings and serve sprinkled liberally with cilantro or parsley.

Buddha's delight

Serves 4

4 oz (125 g) dried rice noodles

8 cups (64 fl oz/2 L) vegetable stock (see page 222)

2 cloves garlic, peeled and chopped

1-inch (2.5-cm) piece fresh ginger, peeled
   and sliced

1 stalk lemongrass or zest (rind) of 1 lime, cut into
   1-inch (2.5-cm) pieces

ground white pepper to taste

1 tablespoon soy sauce or to taste

1 tablespoon lime juice or to taste

8 oz (250 g) pumpkin or butternut squash, cut into
   1-inch (2.5-cm) cubes

4 oz (125 g) green beans

8 ears (cobs) of baby corn

1 carrot, peeled and julienned

1 bunch (13 oz/400 g) baby bok choy, leaves
   separated

1 green bell pepper (capsicum), seeded and sliced

4 oz (125 g) snow peas (mange-tout)

1 tomato, cut into 1-inch (2.5-cm) cubes

2 sprigs fresh herbs, such as basil, cilantro
   (fresh coriander) or chives

4 sprigs mint, for garnish

chili paste or sambal oelek (see page 228), for serving

Bring a large saucepan of water to a boil and add
noodles. Remove from heat and allow to stand until soft,
4–5 minutes. Drain and divide among individual bowls.

Place stock in a large saucepan over medium–high heat,
cover and bring to a boil. Add garlic, ginger, lemongrass,
white pepper, soy sauce and lime juice, reduce heat to
simmer and cook for about 1 minute. Add pumpkin,
beans, corn and carrot and cook until tender–crisp, about
2 minutes. Add bok choy, bell pepper, snow peas, tomato
and herbs and cook until vegetables are tender, about
3 minutes. Ladle over noodles and garnish with mint.
Serve immediately with chili paste.

Burmese vegetable curry

Serves 2

1 tablespoon vegetable oil

1 tablespoon Asian sesame oil

1 onion, chopped

2 tablespoons peeled and grated fresh ginger

4 cloves garlic, finely chopped

2 teaspoons ground turmeric

2 teaspoons dried shrimp paste

1 lb (500 g) mixed vegetables, such as broccoli, cauliflower, beans, zucchini (courgette), and carrots, cut into bite-sized pieces

2 fresh green Thai or Anaheim chilies, seeded and chopped

1¼ cups (10 fl oz/300 ml) coconut milk

In a wok or large skillet, heat oils over medium heat and fry onion, ginger and garlic until onion is soft, about 1 minute. Add turmeric and shrimp paste and fry for 1 minute. Add vegetables and chilies and fry for 5 minutes. Add coconut milk, reduce heat to low and simmer until vegetables are just tender, about 3 minutes. Spoon into serving bowls. Serve with naan bread or steamed jasmine rice.

Chicken and udon noodle salad

Serves 4

2 tablespoons lime juice

2 teaspoons fish sauce (optional)

1 tablespoon mirin

2 teaspoons brown sugar or palm sugar

1 tablespoon peanut oil

1 cup (8 fl oz/250 ml) coconut milk

½ cup (4 fl oz/125 ml) water

2 small red chilies, halved and seeded

1 lemongrass stalk, coarsely chopped, or
   1 teaspoon grated lemon zest (rind)

2 skinless chicken breast fillets

5 oz (150 g) udon noodles or spaghetti

½ red bell pepper (capsicum), seeded and chopped

1 carrot, peeled and grated

3 oz (90 g) snow peas (mange-tout), blanched

1 English (hothouse) cucumber, halved, seeded and
   sliced

3 tablespoons chopped fresh cilantro (fresh
   coriander), plus leaves for garnish

To make dressing, combine lime juice, fish sauce (if using), mirin, sugar and oil in a jar with screw top. Shake well and set aside.

In a saucepan, combine coconut milk, water, chilies, lemongrass or zest and chicken. Bring to a boil, reduce heat to low and simmer until chicken is tender, 7–8 minutes. Remove from heat and allow chicken to cool in liquid.

Drain and discard cooking liquid. Thinly slice chicken.

Cook noodles as directed on package or on page 23. Drain and allow to cool.

In a bowl, combine chicken, noodles, bell pepper, carrot, snow peas, cucumber and chopped cilantro. Mix well. Add dressing and toss until well combined. Cover and refrigerate for 30 minutes to blend flavors.

Spoon onto individual plates and garnish each serving with cilantro leaves.

Chickpea salad with chili and lime dressing

Serves 4

2 tablespoons peanut oil
1 yellow (brown) onion, finely chopped
2 cloves garlic, finely chopped
1⅓ cups (14 oz/440 g) drained, canned chickpeas
juice of 2 limes
¼ cup (2 fl oz/60 ml) chili oil (see page 220)
½ cup (¾ oz/20 g) fresh cilantro (fresh coriander)
  leaves
salt and freshly ground black pepper
crusty bread, warmed, for serving

In a large frying pan or wok over medium heat, heat oil . Add onion and garlic and cook until soft, 3–5 minutes. Add chickpeas and stir until heated through, about 3 minutes. Reduce heat to low, add lime juice and cook, stirring, for 1 minute. Add chili oil and cilantro and season with salt and pepper. Serve warm with bread.

Chili squid salad

Serves 4

8 oz (250 g) rice stick noodles

4 squid (calamari) bodies, about 12 oz (375 g)

2 cups (16 f l oz/500 ml) fish stock (see page 222)

½ cup (4 fl oz/125 ml) dry white wine

1 onion, cut into eights

4 tomatoes, chopped

¼ cup (⅓ oz/10 g) chopped fresh cilantro (fresh coriander)

¼ cup (¾ oz/20 g) chopped fresh mint

¼ cup (1 oz/30 g) chopped scallions (shallots/spring onions)

1–2 small red chilies, seeded, if desired, and halved

3 cloves garlic

1 teaspoon Tabasco sauce

¼ cup (2 fl oz/60 ml) fish sauce

5 tablespoons lime juice

Cook noodles as directed on package or on page 23. Drain and allow to cool.

Cut squid in half lengthwise. Cut shallow slashes in crisscross pattern on inside of squid. Then cut into strips ¾ inch (2 cm) wide. Place stock and wine in saucepan. Bring to a boil, reduce heat to low, add squid and cook until tender, 1–2 minutes. Do not overcook or squid will become tough. Drain and allow to cool.

In a large bowl, combine noodles, squid, onion, tomatoes, cilantro, mint and scallions.

To make dressing, in a food processor, combine chilies to taste, garlic, Tabasco sauce, fish sauce and lime juice. Process until smooth. Set aside until 1 hour before serving.

Add dressing to salad, toss, cover and refrigerate for 1 hour before serving. Divide chilled salad among individual plates.

Crab and lime salad on betel leaves

Serves 6

3 tablespoons fresh lime juice

2 tablespoons coconut vinegar (available from Asian markets)

1 teaspoon Asian sesame oil

1 tablespoon olive oil

2 teaspoons fish sauce

1 lb (500 g) fresh or canned crabmeat, well drained

1 small red chili, seeded and thinly sliced

6 scallions (shallots/spring onions), sliced

2 tablespoons chopped fresh cilantro (fresh coriander)

3 fresh kaffir lime leaves, finely shredded, or
  1 teaspoon grated lime zest (rind)

1/4 cup (1 1/2 oz/45 g) shaved fresh coconut, cut into fine strips

1/4 small English (hothouse) cucumber, seeded and thinly sliced

2 tablespoons chopped fresh Vietnamese mint

12 fresh betel leaves

6 lime wedges, for serving

Place lime juice, vinegar, sesame and olive oils and fish sauce in a screw-top jar. Shake to combine and set aside.

In a bowl, combine crabmeat, chili, scallions, cilantro, lime leaves, coconut, cucumber and mint. Add dressing and gently mix until well combined. Place 2 betel leaves on each plate. Spoon salad onto leaves. Serve with lime wedges.

Tip
Use white vinegar if coconut vinegar is unavailable.

Creamy lentil and split-pea dhal

Serves 3–4

$^2/_3$ cup (5 oz/150 g) lentils, rinsed and drained

$^2/_3$ cup (5 oz/150 g) yellow split peas, rinsed and drained

1 teaspoon ground turmeric

2 fresh green chilies, halved lengthwise

4 teaspoons vegetable oil

1 teaspoon brown or black mustard seeds

1 teaspoon cumin seeds

2 teaspoons garam masala (see page 223)

1 teaspoon ground coriander

$^1/_2$ cup (4 fl oz/125 ml) water

3 tablespoons heavy (double) cream

1 large tomato, unpeeled, chopped

salt to taste

$^1/_4$ cup ($^1/_3$ oz/10 g) chopped fresh cilantro (fresh coriander)

Place lentils and split peas in a bowl and add cold water to cover. Set aside for 30 minutes. Drain.

Fill a large saucepan with water and bring to a boil. Add lentils, split peas, turmeric and chili. Boil, uncovered, until lentils and peas are tender, about 30 minutes. Drain, place in a bowl and mash coarsely. Set aside.

In a saucepan, heat oil over medium–low heat and add mustard seeds. Cook until they crackle, about 30 seconds. Stir in cumin seeds and cook until aromatic, about 30 seconds. Stir in garam masala and coriander. Stir in mashed lentils and peas, water, cream and tomato. Season with salt. Bring to a boil over medium heat, reduce heat to low and simmer, partially covered, stirring often, for 4 minutes. Adjust seasoning. Stir in cilantro and serve hot.

Cumin-flavored potatoes

Serves 4–5

2 lb (1 kg) uniformly sized desiree or pontiac
   potatoes, about 7 medium)

salt as needed

2½ tablespoons cold water

1 teaspoon ground turmeric

½ teaspoon chili powder

¼ cup (2 fl oz/60 ml) vegetable oil and melted
   unsalted butter combined

4 teaspoons cumin seeds

4 teaspoons ground coriander

2 teaspoons finely grated fresh ginger

⅓ cup (½ oz/15 g) chopped fresh cilantro (fresh
   coriander)

juice of ½ lemon

Place potatoes and large pinch salt in a saucepan with enough cold water to cover. Bring to a boil over medium– high heat. Reduce heat to medium–low and cook, partially covered, until potatoes are tender, about 20 minutes. Drain potatoes and let cool for 15 minutes. Peel potatoes and cut into 1½-inch (4-cm) cubes. Set aside.

In a small bowl, combine cold water, turmeric and chili powder and set aside.

In a large, heavy saucepan, heat oil and butter mixture over medium–low heat. Add cumin seeds and cook, stirring, until fragrant, about 30 seconds; take care not to burn seeds. Reduce heat to low and add water and turmeric mixture. Cook, stirring, for 30 seconds. Add potatoes and salt to taste and toss gently until heated through, about 1 minute. Add coriander and toss for 30 seconds. Add ginger and cilantro and toss to combine. Drizzle with lemon juice and serve.

Garlic and cumin lentils

Serves 4

1 cup (7 oz/220 g) masoor dhal (dried red lentils)

²/₃ cup (5 fl oz/150 ml) chicken stock (see page 218) or water

½ teaspoon peeled and finely chopped fresh ginger

½ teaspoon ground coriander

1 tablespoon ghee or vegetable oil

2 teaspoons toasted cumin seeds

1 medium onion (5 oz/150 g), sliced

2 cloves garlic, crushed

1 fresh long green chili, seeded and thinly sliced, (optional)

1 tablespoon finely chopped fresh mint

Place lentils in a sieve and wash under cold running water. Pick over and remove any foreign matter. Soak in water for a minimum of 1 hour. Drain well and place in a dish that will fit in a bamboo steamer or steamer basket. Add stock, ginger and coriander and stir well. Place bowl in steamer.

Partially fill a wok or pot with water (steamer should not touch water) and bring to a rapid simmer. Place steamer over water, cover and steam until lentils are soft, about 30 minutes.

In a medium pan, heat ghee and cook cumin seeds, onion, garlic and chili until onion browns, 8–10 minutes, stirring occasionally. Stir mint and half of onion mixture into lentils. Spread remaining onion mixture on top for garnish. Serve as a dip or side dish with crispy fried pappadams.

Tip

Lentils can be cooked for less time to retain shape (if not being mashed) and used in salads or as a vegetable.

Green beans with lemon miso

Serves 4

2 tablespoons white (shiro) miso

2 tablespoons mirin or sweet white wine

½ teaspoon hot mustard

½ teaspoon grated lemon zest (rind)

8 oz (250 g) green beans, trimmed and halved

2 scallions (shallots/spring onions), green parts only,
    diagonally sliced in ¾-inch (2-cm) lengths

In a small bowl, combine miso, mirin, mustard and lemon zest and mix well. Bring a medium saucepan of water to a boil, add green beans and simmer until just cooked but still crisp, 3–4 minutes, or microwave on high in a covered container with 1 tablespoon water for 2–3 minutes. If serving cold, immediately plunge beans into cold water to prevent further cooking. Toss beans with miso mixture and mix well to combine. Serve hot or cold, garnished with scallions.

Green papaya salad

Serves 4–6

1 lb (500 g) green papaya, peeled and seeded

3 cloves garlic, peeled

10 fresh small green chilies

2 long beans, or about 8 green beans, cut into
 1-inch (2.5-cm) pieces

2 tablespoons dried shrimp

2 tablespoons fish sauce

2 tablespoons fresh lime juice

1 teaspoon palm sugar

1 tablespoon anchovy paste (optional)

1 firm tomato, coarsely chopped, or 5 cherry
 tomatoes, halved

2 tablespoons coarsely ground roasted peanuts

Using a knife or shredder, shred papaya into long, thin strips. You should have about 3 cups (300–350 g); set aside. In a large mortar or bowl, combine garlic, chilies, and beans and pound with a pestle to coarsely bruise. Add papaya and pound again to just bruise ingredients. Add dried shrimp, fish sauce, lime juice and palm sugar. Stir together until sugar has dissolved. Add anchovy paste if using, and tomato. Gently pound to combine flavors. Transfer to a serving platter, sprinkle with peanuts, and serve.

Tip

If unripe or green papaya is unavailable, substitute with shredded, peeled carrot, cucumber or melon.

Jerusalem artichokes with spicy vegetables

Serves 4

8 medium Jerusalem artichokes

2 tablespoons vegetable oil

1 onion, chopped

1 clove garlic, crushed

1 small red chili, seeded and finely chopped

1/2 red bell pepper (capsicum), seeded and finely chopped

1 small green zucchini (courgette), chopped

1 medium tomato, chopped

2 oz (60 g) button mushrooms, sliced

sea salt and freshly ground black pepper to taste

1 tablespoon chopped fresh flat-leaf (Italian) parsley, for garnish

Preheat oven to 350°F (180°C/Gas 4). Prick artichokes several times with a fork. Place on a parchment-lined (baking paper–lined) baking sheet. Bake until soft when pierced with a skewer, about 30 minutes. Time will depend on size of artichokes, as they vary greatly.

About 10 minutes before artichokes are ready, warm oil in a frying pan over medium heat. Add onion, garlic and chili, and cook until onion softens, about 2 minutes. Add bell pepper, zucchini and tomato. Cover and cook over low heat, stirring occasionally, for about 5 minutes. Stir in mushrooms and cook until mushrooms soften, about 1 minute. Add salt and pepper to taste.

Remove artichokes from oven, place on a serving plate and slit open lengthwise.

Top each with 1 tablespoon spicy vegetable mixture and garnish with chopped parsley. Serve remaining vegetable mixture in a bowl.

Mushrooms and corn with cilantro

Serves 4–5

2 ears (cobs) of corn
2 teaspoons unsalted butter
3 tablespoons vegetable oil
1/2-inch (12-mm) cinnamon stick
2 green cardamom pods
2 whole cloves
2 yellow (brown) onions, chopped
1/2 teaspoon salt, plus extra salt to taste
1 teaspoon finely grated fresh ginger
1 teaspoon crushed garlic
1 teaspoon chili powder
1 tablespoon coriander seeds, crushed
1 teaspoon ground turmeric
1 large tomato, unpeeled, finely chopped
1 lb (500 g) small button mushrooms, wiped clean
juice of 1/2 lemon
1/4 cup (1/3 oz/10 g) chopped fresh cilantro (fresh
   coriander)

Use a sharp knife to remove kernels from ears of corn. In
a large saucepan, melt butter over medium–high heat.
Add corn and cook, stirring, until softened, 2–3 minutes.
Remove to a small bowl and set aside.

In same pan, heat oil over medium–low heat. Add
cinnamon, cardamom and cloves and cook, stirring, until
fragrant, about 30 seconds. Add onions and 1/2 teaspoon
salt and cook, uncovered, stirring often, until onions are
dark golden brown, 10–15 minutes.

Add ginger and garlic and cook, stirring, for 30 seconds.
Add chili powder, coriander and turmeric and cook,
stirring, until fragrant, about 30 seconds. Add tomato and
cook, stirring often, until tomato is soft, about 5 minutes.
Add mushrooms and corn and cook, tossing occasionally,
until mushrooms are slightly soft, 5–10 minutes. Add
lemon juice and add salt to taste if necessary. Add cilantro
and toss gently. Serve hot.

Pumpkin and zucchini curry

Serves 4–6

4 cloves garlic, peeled

1-inch (2.5-cm) piece fresh ginger, peeled

1 red (Spanish) onion, coarsely chopped

1 teaspoon ground cumin

1 teaspoon ground coriander

1/2 teaspoon ground cloves

1 teaspoon ground fennel seeds

2 teaspoons Asian sesame oil

2 tablespoons vegetable oil

1–2 small red chilies to taste, seeded and
  finely chopped

2 1/2 cups (20 fl oz/625 ml) thick coconut cream

3 fresh kaffir lime leaves

1 lb (500 g) pumpkin or butternut squash flesh, cut
  into 1-inch (2.5-cm) cubes

4 zucchini (courgettes), cut into 1-inch (2.5-cm) cubes

2 teaspoons fish sauce

2 1/2 cups (2 1/2 oz/75 g) loosely packed baby spinach
  leaves

steamed jasmine rice, for serving

In a small food processor, combine garlic, ginger, onion, cumin, coriander, cloves, fennel seeds and sesame oil. Process until mixture forms a smooth paste, about 20 seconds.

In a wok or large saucepan over medium heat, warm vegetable oil. Add spice paste and chilies and stir-fry until aromatic, 1–2 minutes. Stir in coconut cream, kaffir lime leaves and pumpkin. Cook at a steady simmer over medium–low heat for 10 minutes. Add zucchini and fish sauce and simmer until vegetables are tender, about 10 minutes. Remove curry from heat and gently stir in spinach.

Serve hot with steamed jasmine rice.

Red curry noodles with green vegetables

Serves 4

8 oz (250 g) fresh egg noodles

1½ cups (12 fl oz/375 ml) coconut milk

2½ tablespoons red curry paste (see page 227)

2 tablespoons tamarind pulp

3 teaspoons fish sauce

1 teaspoon superfine (caster) sugar

5 oz (150 g) long beans, trimmed and cut into 2½-inch
  (6-cm) lengths

1 bunch (16 oz/500 g) choy sum, trimmed and leaves
  cut into 2½-inch (6-cm) lengths

2 cups (8 oz/250 g) bean sprouts

⅓ cup (2 oz/60 g) unsalted roasted peanuts

Bring a saucepan of water to a boil. Add noodles and cook until tender, about 3 minutes. (Some precooked noodles need only to be soaked in hot water for 8 minutes; check package for instructions.) Drain noodles and set aside.

In a saucepan over low heat, combine coconut milk, red curry paste, tamarind pulp, fish sauce and sugar. Stir until heated through, about 5 minutes; do not boil. Add beans and choy sum and simmer until vegetables soften slightly, about 3 minutes. Add noodles and bean sprouts and stir until heated through, about 2 minutes. Serve hot, sprinkled with peanuts.

Roasted sweet potato and chili mash

Serves 4–6 as an accompaniment

4 medium sweet potatoes (kumara)
⅓ cup (3 fl oz/90 ml) olive oil
sea salt and freshly ground black pepper to taste
3 teaspoons vegetable oil
1 small red chili, seeded and chopped
2 cloves garlic, crushed
olive oil, for serving

Preheat oven to 400°F (200°C/Gas 6). Place whole, unpeeled sweet potatoes on a parchment-lined (baking paper–lined) baking sheet. Bake until potatoes are tender when pierced with a skewer, 30–40 minutes. Remove from oven and allow to stand until cool enough to handle, 5–10 minutes.

Peel sweet potatoes, place pulp in a bowl and mash until smooth. Gradually beat in olive oil, salt and pepper. Cover and keep warm.

In a small pan over medium heat, heat vegetable oil. Add chili and garlic and cook until aromatic, about 1 minute. Remove from heat and add to potatoes. Mix well.

Serve hot, drizzled with extra olive oil if desired.

Roasted vegetables with Thai herbs

Serves 4–6

1 red bell pepper (capsicum), seeded and quartered
1 yellow bell pepper (capsicum), seeded and
    quartered
3 red (Spanish) onions, peeled and quartered
10 oz (300 g) beets (beetroots), trimmed and quartered
1 lb (500 g) potatoes, quartered
1 lb (500 g) pumpkin or butternut squash, peeled and
    cubed
20 oz (625 g) sweet potato (kumara), peeled and
    cubed
10 oz (300 g) zucchini (courgette), cut into 2-inch
    (5-cm) slices
8 whole cloves garlic, unpeeled
3 lemongrass stalks, cut into 2-inch (5-cm) lengths
4 fresh kaffir lime leaves or 1 tablespoon grated lime
    zest (rind)
½ cup (4 fl oz/120 ml) chili oil (see page 220)
sea salt and freshly ground black pepper
1 cup (8 fl oz/250 ml) fresh lime juice
2 tablespoons chopped fresh cilantro (fresh coriander)
    leaves, for garnish
4 fresh kaffir lime leaves or 1 teaspoon grated lime
    zest (rind), for garnish
crusty bread, for serving
good-quality virgin olive oil, for serving

Preheat oven to 400°F (200°C/Gas 6). Place bell peppers,
onions, beets, potatoes, pumpkin, sweet potato, zucchini,
garlic, lemongrass and 4 lime leaves in a large roasting
pan. Drizzle with chili oil and toss until all vegetables are
coated. Sprinkle liberally with salt and pepper. Bake,
turning 2 or 3 times, until vegetables are tender,
30–40 minutes.

Remove from oven and discard lime leaves and
lemongrass. Arrange vegetables on individual plates.
Drizzle with lime juice and garnish with chopped cilantro
and lime leaves. Accompany with bread and olive oil.

Smoked rainbow trout and chili salad

Serves 2 or 3

$^1/_3$ cup (1$^1/_2$ oz/45 g) unsweetened dried (desiccated)
  shredded coconut

$^3/_4$ cup (6 fl oz/180 ml) water

1$^1/_2$ teaspoons sambal oelek (see page 228)

4 scallions (shallots/spring onions), sliced

1 clove garlic, chopped

$^1/_3$ cup (3 fl oz/90 ml) fresh lime juice

10 oz (300 g) smoked rainbow trout, coarsely
  chopped

2 cups (2 oz/60 g) bean sprouts

1 cup (1 oz/30 g) baby arugula (rocket) leaves,
  chopped

In a small saucepan over medium heat, combine coconut, water, sambal oelek, scallions and garlic. Bring to a boil, stirring, and cook for 2 minutes. Remove from heat and allow to cool completely. Stir in lime juice. Chill until ready to serve.

In a bowl, combine trout, bean sprouts and arugula. Fold in coconut mixture. Serve chilled.

Spiced couscous

Serves 4

2 cups (16 fl oz/500 ml) chicken stock (see page 218)

2 tablespoons olive oil

1 clove garlic, peeled and chopped

1 onion, peeled and chopped

1 small red or green bell pepper (capsicum), seeds
  removed, julienned thinly

½ teaspoon ground cumin

¼ teaspoon ground cinnamon or garam masala (see
  page 223)

½ teaspoon grated orange zest (rind)

freshly ground black pepper

4 dried apricots, chopped

¼ cup (1½ oz/45 g) golden raisins (sultanas)

1 cup (6 oz/180 g) couscous

2 tablespoons chopped fresh cilantro (fresh coriander)

finely julienned orange zest (rind), for garnish (optional)

In a small saucepan over medium–high heat, heat stock.

Meanwhile, in a saucepan over medium heat, heat
1 tablespoon oil. Add garlic, onion and bell pepper and
cook, stirring, until onion is soft, 3–5 minutes. Add hot
stock, spices, zest and black pepper to taste. Bring to a
boil then remove pan from heat.

Add fruit, couscous and cilantro to pan and mix well.
Cover pan and let stand until couscous swells and
absorbs all liquid, about 15 minutes. Serve garnished
with orange zest.

Spiced okra

Serves 4

2 large onions, peeled

3 tablespoons (1½ oz/40 g) butter or margarine

3–4 cloves garlic, crushed

salt and freshly ground black pepper to taste

2 teaspoons ground coriander

½ teaspoon turmeric

1 lb (500 g) okra (ladies fingers), trimmed and cut
  into ½-inch (1-cm) pieces

8 oz (250 g) canned tomatoes

1 teaspoon chopped fresh mint or ½ teaspoon dried
  mint

2 teaspoons tomato paste

½ teaspoon garam masala (see page 223)

Slice 1 of the onions. In a saucepan over medium heat, melt butter. Add sliced onion and fry until soft, about 2 minutes.

In a food processor or blender, liquidize or mince the other onion with the garlic. Add to pan with salt and pepper, coriander and turmeric and cook gently for 5 minutes, stirring occasionally.

Add okra to pan and stir well. Cover pan, reduce heat and simmer very gently for 20 minutes. Add tomatoes, mint, tomato paste and garam masala and continue to simmer gently for 10–15 minutes, stirring occasionally.

Adjust seasonings and serve hot with steamed rice and pappadams.

Spicy tomato rice

Serves 4 as an accompaniment

1 cup (7 oz/220 g) basmati rice

1 tablespoon vegetable oil

1 small onion, chopped

2 cloves garlic, finely chopped

1 fresh red bird's eye or Thai chili, seeded and
    chopped

1 teaspoon cumin seeds

6 black peppercorns

2 whole cloves

1 cinnamon stick

1/2 cup (2 1/2 oz/75 g) fresh or frozen peas

6 1/2 oz (200 g) canned tomatoes

2 tablespoons tomato paste

1 3/4 cups (14 fl oz/440 ml) boiling water

2 tablespoons chopped fresh cilantro (coriander)

sea salt to taste

Rinse rice in several changes of cold water until water
runs clear. Put into a bowl, cover with cold water and let
stand for 5 minutes. Drain and set aside.

In a wok or large, heavy saucepan, heat oil over medium
heat and fry onion, garlic and chili until onion is soft,
1–2 minutes. Add cumin seeds, peppercorns, cloves
and cinnamon stick and cook for 2 minutes. Stir in rice,
peas, tomatoes and tomato paste and cook for
2 minutes, stirring until well combined. Add boiling water,
cover and reduce heat to low. Simmer until rice is tender
and all liquid has been absorbed, 10–12 minutes.
Remove from heat and let stand for 10 minutes. With a
fork, stir in cilantro and salt. Remove whole cloves and
cinnamon stick. Spoon into serving bowls and serve
immediately.

Spicy vegetables on pistachio couscous

Serves 4–6

1 medium (18 oz/550 g) eggplant, cut into ½-inch
(12-mm) pieces
coarse salt, for sprinkling
2–3 tablespoons olive oil
1 large onion, chopped
2 cloves garlic, crushed
½ teaspoon each sweet paprika, ground cardamom,
cumin, turmeric and cinnamon
2 medium tomatoes, chopped
10 oz (300 g) canned chickpeas, drained
6 cups (1½ lb/750 g) thickly sliced mixed zucchini
(courgette), carrots, cauliflower florets and green
beans
2 tablespoons chopped mixed fresh herbs such as
parsley, mint and fresh cilantro (fresh coriander)
¾ cup (6 fl oz/180 ml) vegetable stock (see
page 222)
1 cup (6 oz/185 g) instant couscous
1½ cups (12 fl oz/375 ml) chicken stock (see
page 218)
2 oz (60 g) butter, melted, or olive oil
½ cup (2 oz/60 g) pistachios, toasted and chopped
fresh parsley, for garnish

Sprinkle eggplant with salt and let stand 30 minutes.
Rinse under cold water, drain and pat dry with paper
towels.

In a large saucepan, heat oil and sauté eggplant, onion
and garlic until onion is softened but not brown, about
5 minutes. Add spices, tomatoes, chickpeas,
vegetables, herbs and vegetable stock to pan, cover and
simmer until vegetables are tender and flavors are well
blended, 20–25 minutes.

In a small saucepan, heat chicken stock then remove
from heat and stir in couscous. Let stand until all liquid is
absorbed, 4–5 minutes. Stir in butter or olive oil so
couscous is evenly coated. Break up any lumps and
spread couscous in a bamboo steamer or steamer
basket lined with parchment (baking) paper then cover.
Place over vegetables and steam for last 10–15 minutes
of cooking time to heat through. Stir in pistachios.

Serve couscous topped with vegetables and garnished
with parsley.

Tip
To toast pistachios: Remove shells and place pistachios
under a broiler (grill) or in a dry frying pan over medium
heat and cook, stirring, until they just change color,
3–4 minutes. Be careful not to burn them.

Stuffed zucchini

Serves 2

1 long, thin zucchini (courgette)
4½ teaspoons table salt
1½ cups (12 fl oz/375 ml) water
3 dried Chinese mushrooms, soaked for 30 minutes
   in several changes of water
5 oz (150 g) ground (minced) beef
vegetable or sunflower oil, for frying
1 egg, separated
1 tablespoon Korean soy sauce
1 tablespoon sugar
¼ cup (2 fl oz/60 ml) beef stock
pinch of shredded red chilies

For beef and mushroom marinade
2 tablespoons light soy sauce
1 tablespoon sugar
4 teaspoons finely chopped scallions (shallots/spring
   onions)
2 teaspoons crushed garlic
2 teaspoons sesame oil
2 teaspoons pan-toasted, ground sesame seeds
freshly ground black pepper to taste

Cut zucchini diagonally into pieces 1½ inches (4 cm) long. Make a lengthwise slit through each piece to within about ¼ inch (6 mm) of each end. Combine salt and water and soak zucchini pieces for about 30 minutes.

Meanwhile, squeeze excess water from mushrooms. Remove and discard stems, and finely chop caps.

To make beef and mushroom marinade: In a glass or ceramic bowl, combine beef and mushroom marinade ingredients. Add ground beef and mushroom slices to marinade and set aside to marinate, 20–30 minutes.

In a frying pan over medium heat, heat oil and fry egg white and yolk separately, to make two omelettes. Remove from pan and slice into thin strips.

In a frying pan over high heat, heat 1 tablespoon oil and stir-fry the marinated beef and mushrooms for 2–3 minutes.

Remove zucchini from salted water. Gently squeeze out excess water, then drain on paper towels. Press beef and mushroom mixture into slits in zucchini.

In a saucepan, combine soy sauce, sugar and beef stock and bring to a boil. Add stuffed zucchini and boil for 1 minute. Reduce heat and simmer until zucchini is tender, 2–3 minutes.

Serve on a deep plate, garnished with omelette strips and shredded red chili.

Thai beef salad

Serves 4

2 tablespoons soy sauce

2 cloves garlic, crushed

1 tablespoon rice wine

1 lb (500 g) sirloin (rump) steak

2 tablespoons olive oil

4 oz (125 g) thin egg noodles

4 oz (125 g) green beans, trimmed and blanched

½ English (hothouse) cucumber, seeded and thinly
  sliced

3 small red chilies, seeded and sliced

2 tablespoons chopped fresh cilantro (fresh coriander)

2 tablespoons fresh mint leaves

1 cup (4 oz/125 g) fresh bean spouts or mung beans,
  rinsed

1 cup (4 oz/125 g) unsalted roasted peanuts

2 tablespoons lime juice

2 tablespoons fish sauce

1 clove garlic, crushed

1 tablespoon palm sugar or brown sugar

In a glass or ceramic bowl, combine soy sauce, garlic and rice wine. Add steak and turn to coat with marinade. Cover and marinate for 30 minutes. Drain steak and pat dry with paper towels.

In a frying pan over high heat, warm oil. When hot, add steak and cook until light brown on outside and rare on inside, about 2 minutes on each side. Allow steak to cool, then thinly slice across grain and set aside.

Cook noodles as directed on package or on page 23. Drain and allow to cool.

In a bowl, combine steak, noodles, green beans, cucumber, chilies, cilantro, mint, bean sprouts or mung beans and peanuts.

Place lime juice, fish sauce, garlic and palm or brown sugar into a jar with screw top. Shake well and set aside dressing until just before serving.

Add dressing to salad, toss gently and serve.

Tofu with vegetables, chili and sesame

Serves 4

2 tablespoons oyster sauce

1 tablespoon water

2 teaspoons soy sauce

2 tablespoons vegetable oil

2 cloves garlic, finely chopped

2 teaspoons peeled and grated fresh ginger

2 small red bird's eye of serrano chilies, seeded
  and thinly sliced

1 red bell pepper (capsicum), seeded and sliced

1 bunch choy sum, about 16 oz (500 g), trimmed and
  cut into 2½-inch (6-cm) lengths

8 long beans, trimmed and cut into 2½-inch (6-cm)
  lengths

5 oz (150 g) deep-fried tofu puffs, cut into 1-inch
  (2.5-cm) cubes

3 teaspoons toasted sesame seeds, for garnish

In a small bowl, combine oyster sauce, water and soy sauce. In a wok over medium heat, warm vegetable oil. Add garlic, ginger and chilies and stir-fry until aromatic, 1–2 minutes. Add bell pepper, choy sum and beans and stir-fry until slightly softened, 2–3 minutes. Add tofu and oyster sauce mixture. Toss until tofu and vegetables are well coated and tofu is heated through, 3–4 minutes. Serve hot, garnished with sesame seeds.

Tip

If deep-fried tofu puffs are unavailable, fry your own tofu pieces. To fry tofu pieces: Cut 6½ oz (200 g) firm tofu into 1-inch (2.5-cm) cubes. In a wok over medium heat, warm ¼ cup (2 fl oz/60 ml) vegetable oil. Working in batches, add tofu and stir-fry until golden on all sides, 2–3 minutes. Using a slotted spoon, remove from wok and drain on paper towels.

Tuna and red onion salad

Serves 4

Dressing

1 small red chili, seeded, if desired, and thinly
 sliced, or 1 teaspoon chili sauce

1 clove garlic, crushed

grated zest (rind) of 1 lime

1 tablespoon lime juice

2 tablespoons olive oil

1 tablespoon balsamic vinegar

Salad

6½ oz (200 g) rice stick, somen, udon or soba
 noodles

6 oz (185 g) canned tuna in oil, drained and flaked

1 red onion, chopped

¼ cup (⅓ oz/10 g) chopped fresh cilantro (fresh
 coriander)

To make dressing, place chili, garlic, lime zest and juice,
olive oil and vinegar in a jar with screw top. Shake well
and set aside.

To make salad, cook noodles as directed on package or
on page 23. Drain and allow to cool.

In a bowl, combine noodles, tuna, onion and cilantro.
Mix well.

Add dressing and toss until well combined. Cover and
refrigerate for 30 minutes to blend flavors.

Spoon into individual bowls and serve chilled.

Vegetable and tofu Thai green curry

Serves 4

1 tablespoon soybean oil

2–3 tablespoons green curry paste (see page 227)

5 shallots (French shallots) or 1 yellow (brown) onion, chopped

6 cups (20 oz/600 g) pumpkin or butternut squash, peeled and cut into ³⁄₄-inch (2-cm) cubes

5 oz (150 g) firm or fresh tofu, cut into ³⁄₄-inch (2-cm) cubes

3 baby eggplants (aubergines), about 6 oz (180 g) total, diced

2¹⁄₄ cups (18 fl oz/560 ml) coconut milk

10 small deep-fried tofu puffs

4 fresh kaffir lime leaves, finely sliced

2 cups (10 oz/300 g) fresh or frozen soybeans

3¹⁄₂ oz (105 g) green beans, cut into 1-inch (2.5-cm) lengths

¹⁄₃ cup (¹⁄₂ oz/15 g) shredded fresh basil leaves

1 tablespoon fresh lime juice

1 tablespoon fish sauce

1 teaspoon palm or brown sugar

In a large frying pan, heat oil over medium heat and cook curry paste and shallots until fragrant, about 2 minutes. Add pumpkin, tofu and eggplant and cook, stirring, for 2 minutes. Add coconut milk, deep-fried tofu and lime leaves and simmer for 10 minutes. Add soybeans and green beans and simmer for 5 minutes. Add basil, lime juice, fish sauce and sugar and stir until sugar dissolves. Serve with steamed rice.

Vegetables in spiced yogurt

Serves 4–6

1¼ cups (10 fl oz/300 ml) water
4 large fresh green chilies, quartered lengthwise
18 fresh curry leaves
½ teaspoon ground turmeric
1 large desiree potato, cut into 2-inch (5-cm) sticks
1 large carrot, cut into 2-inch (5-cm) sticks
1 yellow (brown) onion, cut into very thin wedges
1 baby eggplant (aubergine), cut into 2-inch (5-cm) sticks
1 large zucchini (courgette), cut into 2-inch (5-cm) sticks
4 oz (125 g) green beans, trimmed and cut into 2-inch (5-cm) lengths

Spiced yogurt
½ cup (4 oz/125 g) plain (natural) whole-milk yogurt
½ teaspoon ground coriander
½ teaspoon ground cumin
¼ teaspoon ground black pepper
salt to taste

In a large saucepan, combine water, chilies, curry leaves and turmeric and bring to a boil over medium–high heat. Add potato, carrot, onion, eggplant, zucchini and beans and mix well. Cover, reduce heat to medium–low and simmer, stirring occasionally, until vegetables are just tender, about 15 minutes.

While vegetables cook, make spiced yogurt. In a bowl, combine yogurt, coriander, cumin, pepper and salt and mix well.

Drain all but about 1½ tablespoons liquid from vegetables. Add spiced yogurt and mix gently over very low heat until combined. Do not overheat or yogurt may separate. Serve hot.

desserts

Bananas in coconut milk

Serves 4

8 unpeeled, small, slightly green, sugar bananas or
  4–6 standard-sized bananas
4 cups (32 fl oz/1 L) coconut milk
2 pandan (screwpine) leaves, bruised and tied into a
  knot, or 2 drops pandan extract
2 tablespoons palm sugar
¼ cup (2 oz/60 g) granulated (white) sugar
pinch of salt

Cook bananas in a covered steamer over rapidly
simmering water until skin begins to break, about
5 minutes. Or, cook bananas in a pot of boiling water for
about 2 minutes. Remove bananas from heat, let cool
slightly, then carefully peel. Cut each banana into quarters;
once lengthwise, then across.

Let coconut milk stand, allowing thick coconut milk to rise
to the top. Spoon about 2 cups (16 fl oz/500 ml) thick
coconut milk into a bowl and reserve.

In a large saucepan over medium–high heat, combine
remaining thin coconut milk and pandan leaves or extract.
Bring to a boil and add banana pieces, both sugars and
salt. Add thick coconut milk, bring to a boil and reduce
heat to simmer gently for about 3 minutes. Remove from
heat. Serve either hot or cold in individual bowls.

Tips

• Slightly green bananas work best here, as they are less
likely to break up during poaching. Other alternatives
include peeled and cubed pumpkin, squash, sweet potato
(kumara) or taro—steam or boil until just tender, and cook
as above, until tender.

• Hard or loaf palm sugar is preferred in this recipe as it
contains tapioca starch which slightly thickens the sauce.

Black sticky rice pudding

Serves 4–6

1 cup (7 oz/220 g) black sticky (glutinous) rice

3½ cups (28 fl oz/875 ml) water

1 cup (8 fl oz/250 ml) coconut cream, plus ¼ cup
(2 fl oz/60 ml) extra

¼ cup (2 oz/60 g) granulated (white) sugar

In a medium saucepan over medium–high heat, combine rice and water and bring to a boil. Reduce heat to simmer, and cook until tender, about 30 minutes, stirring occasionally at the beginning and frequently towards the end. Add additional water if necessary. Once rice is just tender and grains begin to open, add 1 cup (8 fl oz/250 ml) coconut cream and sugar. Stir well and cook for a further few minutes. Remove from heat. To serve, spoon pudding into individual bowls and drizzle with extra ¼ cup (2 fl oz/60 ml) coconut cream.

Tip

This recipe can be served hot, at room temperature or chilled, but it is best when eaten on the day it is made.

Carrot and cardamom milk pudding

Serves 10

2 lb (1 kg) carrots, about 9 medium, peeled and
   grated

8 cups (64 fl oz/2 L) whole (full cream) milk

3 tablespoons green cardamom pods

6–8 saffron threads

½ cup (4 fl oz/125 ml) whole (full cream) milk, heated

½ cup (2 oz/60 g) sliced (flaked) almonds

½ cup (2 oz/60 g) pistachio nuts, sliced

1 cup (8 oz/250 g) sugar

⅓ cup (2 oz/60 g) raisins

⅔ cup (5 oz/150 g) ghee or unsalted butter

Preheat oven to 350°F (180°C/Gas 4).

In a large, heavy saucepan, combine carrots and 8 cups milk and bring to a boil over medium–high heat. Reduce heat to medium and cook, uncovered, stirring often, until most of milk is absorbed and carrots are soft, about 1¼ hours.

While carrots are cooking, grind cardamom to a powder in a spice grinder. Set aside.

In a bowl, combine saffron and hot milk and set aside for 10 minutes.

Spread almonds and pistachios on a baking sheet and toast in oven, stirring nuts occasionally, for 6–8 minutes. Remove from oven and let cool.

Add cardamom, saffron mixture, sugar and raisins to carrot mixture and cook, stirring, until sugar dissolves. Simmer, uncovered, stirring often, until all liquid is absorbed, about 45 minutes.

Add ghee or butter, a spoonful at a time, stirring until combined. Cook, stirring often, until pudding begins to pull away from sides of pan, 10–15 minutes. Stir in three-fourths of nuts. Spoon into bowls and sprinkle with remaining nuts. Serve warm.

Tip

You can spread pudding evenly in a shallow 8-inch (20-cm) square baking pan lined with plastic wrap. Refrigerate until cold. Use plastic wrap to lift pudding from pan. Cut pudding into individual portions to serve.

Cottage cheese dumplings in syrup

Serves 10

Syrup
4 cups (2 lb/1 kg) sugar
4 cups (32 fl oz/1 L) water
1 green cardamom pod, cracked
small pinch of saffron threads

Dumplings
2 cups (6 oz/180 g) whole (full cream) powdered milk
1 cup (5 oz/150 g) all-purpose (plain) flour
1/4 teaspoon ground cardamom
about 1 cup (8 fl oz/250 ml) heavy (double) cream
6 cups (48 fl oz/1.5 L) vegetable oil

To make syrup: In a large saucepan, combine sugar, water, cardamom pod and saffron. Stir over low heat until sugar dissolves. Keep warm over low heat.

To make dumplings: In a large bowl, combine powdered milk, flour and ground cardamom. Add cream and, using your hands, gradually incorporate flour mixture into cream to form a soft dough, adding a little more cream if dough is a bit dry. Knead lightly in bowl until smooth. Shape mixture into 20 walnut-sized balls, making sure surface of each ball is very smooth. If necessary, brush balls very lightly with water and smooth over any cracks.

In a large saucepan, heat oil over medium heat to 350°F (180°C) on a deep-frying thermometer. Fry dumplings in four batches in hot oil, gently stirring them occasionally with a large slotted spoon (do not marr surface), until uniformly golden brown, 3–5 minutes. Remove to paper towels to drain for 2 minutes, then add to warm syrup. Soak in syrup for at least 30 minutes. Serve warm.

Tip
Always serve two or more dumplings per person as it is considered rude to offer only one.

Ginger and lychee granita

Serves 4–6

11 oz (330 g) canned lychees (litchis) in syrup (see
  Tips)
¼ cup (½ oz/15 g) candied (crystallized) ginger,
  chopped
⅔ cup (5 fl oz/150 ml) water
2 teaspoons freshly squeezed lemon or lime juice
mint sprigs, for garnish

Pour lychees and their syrup into a blender or food
processor (see Tips). Add ginger, water and lemon juice,
then process until coarsely pureed. Pour into a shallow
pan or ice tray and place in freezer. Stir every
15 minutes until mixture freezes. To serve, use a heavy
spoon to scrape granita crystals into a bowl. Garnish
with mint sprigs.

Tips

• Most canned lychees are already pitted; if not, cut
away and discard seed from each fruit before pureeing.

• To use fresh lychees, remove both peel and pit and
add ½ cup (4 fl oz/125 ml) sugar syrup (see page 211).

• Candied ginger comes both crystallized and in syrup;
both varieties suit this recipe. If in season, mild-tasting
young ginger, with a pale, parchmentlike skin, can
replace the candied ginger. Older ginger, with a darker,
thicker skin, does not suit as it is more fibrous and
stronger tasting.

• Granita is a sweetened ice, coarser in texture than
sherbet (sorbet) or ice cream. If using an ice cream
machine, add ½ egg white to mixture and process as
above. The granita will be lighter in both color and
texture.

Mango ice cream

Serves 10

1 ripe mango, about 12 oz (360 g), peeled, pitted and
  coarsely chopped

1½ tablespoons green cardamom pods

1⅔ cups (13 fl oz/400 ml) sweetened condensed
  milk

3 cups (24 fl oz/750 ml) heavy (double) cream

Rich sauce (see page 201), for serving

Extra ripe mango, peeled, pitted and thinly sliced, for
  serving (optional)

In a food processor, puree mango until smooth. Remove
to a large bowl. In a spice grinder, grind cardamom to a
powder and add to mango.

Add condensed milk and cream to mango mixture and
stir until well combined; do not beat or whisk. Divide
mixture among 10 ramekins with a ½-cup (4-fl oz/125-ml)
capacity. Place in freezer until frozen, about 6 hours.
Cover ramekins tightly and keep in freezer until serving.

To serve, briefly dip each ramekin in a bowl of hot water.
Invert a serving plate on top and invert plate and ramekin
to unmold ice cream. Top with sauce and serve
immediately, decorated with thin slices of extra ripe
mango, if desired.

Tips

You can make ice cream up to 2 weeks ahead. Wrap
well to prevent flavors being absorbed from other foods
in freezer. Make sauce close to serving.

Pistachio and cardamom ice cream

Serves 4

½ cup (3½ oz/105 g) superfine (caster) sugar

5 cardamom pods, bruised

3 cups (24 fl oz/750 ml) evaporated milk

¾ cup (6 fl oz/180 ml) thickened cream or heavy
   (double) cream

1 cup (4 oz/125 g) shelled pistachio nuts, finely
   chopped

slices of fresh mango, for serving (optional)

In a heavy-bottomed saucepan, combine sugar, cardamom pods, evaporated milk and cream. Place over medium heat and stir for 10 minutes; do not allow to boil. Remove from heat and stir in pistachio nuts. Allow mixture to cool to room temperature. Pour mixture into four 1-cup (8-fl oz/250-ml) molds and freeze overnight. Remove ice cream from molds and serve with slices of fresh mango if desired.

Tip

Disposable paper cups make good molds for ice cream. After the ice cream freezes, the cups can be peeled away easily.

In a bowl, combine saffron and hot milk and set aside for 10 minutes. Place pistachio nuts in a food processor and process until finely chopped. In a spice grinder, grind cardamom to a powder.

Place condensed milk and cream in a bowl. Stir until well combined; do not whisk or beat. Add pistachio nuts, saffron and milk mixture and ground cardamom. Stir until well combined.

Divide mixture among 10 ramekins with a 1/2-cup (4-fl oz/125-ml) capacity. Place in freezer until ice cream is frozen, about 6 hours. Cover ramekins tightly and keep in freezer until serving.

To make sauce: In a saucepan, combine sugar, cream and star anise. Stir over low heat until sugar dissolves. Bring to a boil, reduce heat to low and cook, uncovered, stirring often, until sauce thickens slightly, about 10 minutes.

To serve, briefly dip each ramekin in a bowl of hot water. Invert a serving plate on top and invert plate and ramekin to unmold ice cream. Top with sauce and serve immediately.

Tips

You can make ice cream up to 2 weeks ahead. Wrap well to prevent flavors being absorbed from other foods in freezer. Make sauce close to serving.

Saffron and pistachio ice cream

Serves 10

large pinch of saffron threads
1/2 cup (4 fl oz/125 ml) milk, heated
1/3 cup (3 1/2 oz/105 g) pistachio nuts
3 tablespoons green cardamom pods
1 2/3 cups (13 fl oz/400 ml) sweetened condensed milk
3 cups (24 fl oz/750 ml) heavy (double) cream

Rich sauce
1/2 cup (4 oz/125 g) raw or demarara sugar
1/2 cup (4 fl oz/125 ml) heavy (double) cream
5 star anise

Steamed banana cake

Makes 1 cake

3 cups (12 oz/375 g) grated fresh coconut or
  unsweetened dried (desiccated) shredded coconut
5 ripe bananas, about 1½ lb (750 g) in total, peeled
  and mashed
1 cup (5 oz/150 g) rice flour or very finely ground rice
¼ cup (1 oz/30 g) tapioca starch
1½ cups (12 oz/375 g) granulated (white) sugar
½ teaspoon salt
½ cup (4 fl oz/125 ml) coconut cream

If using unsweetened dried coconut, soak first in cold
water for 10 minutes, then squeeze dry. Reserve one-
fourth of coconut for garnish.

In a medium bowl, mash bananas then stir in all remaining
ingredients except reserved coconut. Lightly oil an 8-inch
x 10-inch (20-cm x 25-cm) cake pan. Pour in cake mixture
and smooth top. Sprinkle with reserved coconut. Cover
tightly with plastic wrap or lay a banana leaf on top. Place
the cake in a steamer, or on a wire rack in a wok, over
gently boiling water. Make sure water does not touch cake
pan. Cover steamer, and steam for 30 minutes. Cake will
be slightly springy to the touch when done.

Remove pan from heat, and drain away any accumulated
water. Let cool completely, then cut into small squares and
carefully remove pieces with a spatula. Serve warm or at
room temperature.

Tip

Standard servings of this cake may prove too large and
heavy, so the smaller the servings, the better.

Sweet black bean "soup"

Serves 6

1 cup (7 oz/220 g) dried small black beans or black-eyed peas
8 cups (64 fl oz/2 L) water, for cooking
1 tablespoon arrowroot or tapioca starch
1 cup (8 oz/250 g) sugar
crushed ice

To pre-soak beans: If using black beans or black-eyed peas (beans), soak overnight or for at least four hours. Alternatively, for a quick soaking method, place beans or peas in a medium pot with a tight-fitting lid. Cover with water and bring to a boil, uncovered, for 1 minute. Remove from heat, cover tightly and rest for 1 hour. Drain before using.

In a large pot, combine beans and water. Bring to a boil, reduce heat and simmer until beans are barely tender, up to 1½ hours. (Surprisingly, these tiny black beans cook much slower than other beans, yet still retain crunchiness.)

Take a spoonful or so of cooking juices and stir into arrowroot, then add to pot. Add sugar and stir to dissolve. Remove from heat and let cool. Refrigerate until chilled, at least 2 hours. Spoon beans and juice into individual glasses or cups, add some crushed ice and serve.

Tips

• Sweetened condensed milk can be used to sweeten this recipe.

• Substitute beans with black gram (sabat urad), available at Asian markets, some natural foods stores, and Indian markets. If using black gram, do not pre-soak, and cook for about 30 minutes only.

Sweet gingered rice

Serves 4–6

1 cup (6½ oz/200 g) uncooked sticky (glutinous) rice

½ cup (4 oz/125 g) raw sugar or palm sugar, preferably dark

¾ cup (6 fl oz/180 ml) water

1-inch (2.5-cm) piece fresh ginger, peeled and finely grated

½ cup (2 oz/60 g) fresh or unsweetened dried (desiccated) grated coconut

2 tablespoons chopped peanuts, lightly toasted

Soak rice in water to cover for at least 3 hours and preferably for 8 hours; drain. Pour into a conical bamboo steamer or steamer basket lined with cheesecloth (muslin). Set over a pot of boiling water, cover and steam until tender, about 20 minutes. Turn out rice into a medium bowl. Cover and keep warm.

In a small saucepan over high heat, combine sugar and water. Stir until dissolved, then boil for 1 minute. Add ginger. Reduce heat and barely simmer for 5 minutes. Pour syrup over cooked rice. Stir lightly until rice is just coated. As it will set while cooling, spoon rice immediately into small individual bowls or molds. Alternatively, flatten into a tray or plate and cut into large 1¼-inch (3-cm) cubes. Serve at room temperature, garnished with coconut and peanuts.

Tip

If using fresh coconut, see page 219 for preparation. You will only need a small quantity for this recipe, so wrap and refrigerate remainder for another use, such as to make coconut milk.

Sweet sticky rice with mango

Serves 4–6

4 cups (28 oz/875 g) sticky (glutinous) rice

2 cups (16 fl oz/500 ml) coconut cream

1 cup (8 oz/250 g) granulated (white) sugar plus
  2 tablespoons extra

½ teaspoon salt plus pinch extra

½ cup (4 fl oz/125 ml) coconut milk

2–3 fresh mangoes, peeled, pitted and
  thinly sliced

1 tablespoon sesame seeds, lightly toasted

Place sticky rice in a large, deep bowl and add water to cover by 2 inches (5 cm). Soak for at least 3 hours, preferably 8 hours. Drain, then pour rice into a conical bamboo steamer or steamer basket lined with cheesecloth (muslin). If available, place a small round bamboo mat, about 6 inches (15 cm) in diameter, into the bottom of the basket (this facilitates removal and cleaning later). Set basket over a steamer pot filled with boiling water. The basket should fit snugly deep inside the pot, but not touch the water. Cover and steam until grains are tender, about 20 minutes. Halfway through cooking, toss rice so that it is upended. It should have already formed into a cohesive ball by this point.

In a large bowl, stir together coconut cream, sugar and ½ teaspoon salt. Add hot rice, stirring until grains are well coated. Let cool completely at room temperature. (Do not refrigerate or the rice will harden.) The rice will absorb all the coconut liquid; stir occasionally. Meanwhile, in a small bowl, combine coconut milk, extra sugar and pinch of salt.

When ready to serve, divide sticky rice among individual serving bowls. Lay mango slices on top of sticky rice. Pour coconut milk mixture over mangoes and sprinkle with sesame seeds.

Tip

If fresh mango is unavailable, use canned mango, drained.

drinks

Chai Indian tea

Serves 8

4 cups (32 fl oz/1 L) cold water
4 teaspoons finely grated fresh ginger
$1/3$ cup (1 oz/30 g) tea leaves
3 tablespoons milk, plus milk for serving
$1/2$ teaspoon garam masala (see page 223)
sugar to taste

In a saucepan, combine water and ginger and bring to a boil over medium heat. Reduce heat and stir in tea leaves. Bring to a boil again and stir in 3 tablespoons milk and garam masala.

Remove from heat and cover pan. Set aside for 4 minutes. Strain and add sugar to taste. Serve with extra milk.

Tips

Indians generally drink their chai strong with lots of milk and sugar, but you can vary the amounts depending on how strong or diluted you like your chai. As a variation, use ground cardamom instead of garam masala.

Chilled spiced tea

Serves 6–8

2 long red chilies, halved

2 lemongrass stalks, sliced

2-inch (5-cm) piece fresh ginger, peeled and sliced

1/4 cup (2 oz/60 g) brown sugar

4 cups (32 fl oz/1 L) boiling water

6–8 sprigs fresh Vietnamese mint

crushed ice (optional)

In a heatproof pitcher, combine chilies, lemongrass, ginger and brown sugar. Add boiling water and steep for 5 minutes. Strain into a porcelain or glass teapot. Refrigerate for 1 hour or more.

To serve, place mint sprigs into small serving glasses and add chilled tea. Add crushed ice if desired.

Chilled yogurt drink (Lassi)

Serves 10

pinch of saffron threads
$^2/_3$ cup (5 fl oz/150 ml) milk, heated
3 tablespoons green cardamom pods
8 cups (4 lb/2 kg) plain (natural) whole-milk yogurt
$^1/_2$ cup (3$^1/_2$ oz/105 g) superfine (caster) sugar
crushed ice, for serving

In a bowl, combine saffron and warm milk and set aside
for 10 minutes. In a spice grinder, grind cardamom to a
powder.

In a large bowl, combine saffron mixture, cardamom,
yogurt and sugar. Whisk thoroughly until sugar dissolves
and mixture begins to froth.

Pour into glasses, add crushed ice and serve immediately.

Tip
You can thin lassi by adding milk.

Fresh lemon or lime soda

Serves 1–2

$\frac{1}{3}$ cup (3 fl oz/90 ml) freshly squeezed lemon or lime juice
$\frac{1}{3}$ cup (3 fl oz/90 ml) sugar syrup (see below), plus more to taste if required
pinch of salt (optional)
ice cubes
about 1 cup (8 fl oz/250 ml) soda water or water

In a glass, combine lime juice, sugar syrup and salt, if using. Pour into a glass tumbler packed with ice. Add soda water to fill and add more sugar syrup to taste, if desired.

Sugar syrup

Makes 1$\frac{1}{4}$ cups (10 fl oz/300 ml)

1 cup (8 oz/250 g) sugar
1 cup (8 fl oz/250 ml) water

In a medium saucepan, combine sugar and water. Cook over low heat, stirring until sugar dissolves. Stop stirring, increase heat to high and bring to a boil. Cook for 3 minutes without stirring. To prevent syrup from crystallizing, brush pan side with cold water. Remove from heat and let cool completely. Pour into a jar, cover and refrigerate indefinitely.

Variation: Vanilla sugar syrup Add 1 vanilla bean, split lengthwise, to sugar syrup after removing it from heat. Alternatively, stir in $\frac{1}{4}$ teaspoon vanilla extract (essence).

Green mango drink

Serves 10

2 lb (1 kg) unripe green mangoes
3 tablespoons green cardamom pods
½ cup (4 oz/125 g) sugar
pinch salt
8 cups (64 fl oz/2 L) ice-cold water
crushed ice, for serving

Rinse mangoes and place in a large saucepan. Add enough water to cover and bring to a simmer over medium heat. Cook, partially covered, until mangoes are soft and mushy, 20–30 minutes. Drain and reserve cooking water. Set mangoes aside to cool.

In a spice grinder, grind cardamom to a powder. Set aside.

Remove mango pulp from skins and pits. Place pulp in a blender with cardamom, sugar and salt. Puree until smooth, adding some cooking water if necessary to facilitate blending.

Remove mango puree to a bowl and combine with ice-cold water. Taste and adjust sugar and salt if necessary. Pour into tall glasses and add crushed ice. Serve immediately.

Tip

As a variation, omit cardamom and add 1 teaspoon ground, dry-roasted cumin seeds and a handful of fresh mint leaves.

Mango and cumin lassi

Serves 4

$^{3}/_{4}$ teaspoon cumin seeds

1$^{1}/_{4}$ cups (10 oz/300 g) plain (natural) whole-milk
  yogurt

1$^{1}/_{4}$ cups (10 fl oz/300 ml) non-fat milk

1 ripe mango, peeled, pitted and chopped

superfine (caster) sugar to taste

crushed ice, for serving

In a nonstick pan over medium heat, toast cumin seeds
until aromatic, 1–2 minutes. Remove from pan and allow
to cool.

In a food processor, combine $^{1}/_{2}$ teaspoon cumin seeds,
yogurt, milk and mango and process until thick.
Sweeten to taste with sugar. Place a handful of crushed
ice into each glass. Pour lassi over ice. Serve
immediately, sprinkled lightly with remaining cumin
seeds.

sauces, stocks and condiments

Front: Adjat sauce; center: Chili jam; back: Sweet chili relish

Adjat sauce

Makes about ³/₄ cup (6 fl oz/180 ml)

¹/₃ cup (3 oz/90 g) granulated (white) sugar

¹/₃ cup (3 fl oz/90 ml) water

2 tablespoons rice vinegar

¹/₄ cup (2 oz/60 g) peeled, thinly sliced cucumber

1¹/₂ tablespoons ground roasted peanuts

1 tablespoon thinly sliced shallots (French shallots),
   preferably pink

1 tablespoon coarsely chopped fresh cilantro
   (coriander) leaves and stems

¹/₄ fresh long red chili, coarsely chopped

In a small saucepan over low heat, combine sugar and
water and stir until sugar dissolves. Increase heat, bring
syrup to a full boil and cook without stirring for a few
minutes. Remove from heat and let cool. Stir remaining
ingredients into syrup and serve.

Tip

This sauce traditionally accompanies both massaman and
yellow curries, although it is rarely served in restaurants
today. It may also be served with meat satay, but if doing
so, omit the peanuts.

Chili jam

Makes about 1³/₄ cups (14 fl oz/440 ml)

2 whole bulbs garlic
4 oz (125 g) shallots (French shallots), preferably
  pink
15 dried long red chilies
1 cup (8 fl oz/250 ml) vegetable oil
2 tablespoons palm sugar
1 tablespoon granulated (white) sugar
¹/₄ teaspoon salt

Preheat oven to 400°F (200°C/Gas 6). Lightly break unpeeled garlic bulb by pressing on a knife handle with the heel of your hand, so that the cloves sit loosely together; do not separate cloves from bulb completely. Separately wrap garlic and shallots in aluminum foil. Roast on top shelf of oven until soft to touch, about 30 minutes. Remove from oven and allow to cool in foil. Peel shallots and garlic.

Roast chilies by tossing them in a wok or large, heavy frying pan over high heat until lightly brown, 2–3 minutes. Remove stems, but retain seeds. In a large mortar, grind chilies to a powder with a pestle. Add roasted garlic and shallots and pound until smooth. (Or, place chilies in a food processor to grind, then add garlic and shallots and process until smooth.)

In a wok or large, heavy frying pan over medium heat, heat oil and add chili paste. Reduce heat to low and cook for about 5 minutes, stirring frequently. Add sugars and salt, and stir until dissolved. Remove from heat.

Store in a covered jar for up to 6 months in the refrigerator. Do not drain off any oil from the top, as this helps to preserve the jam.

Tip
Chili jam is served in Thailand as a table condiment, much like ketchup and mustard in the West.

Sweet chili relish

Makes about 5 cups (36 fl oz/1.25 L)

2 cups (8 oz/250 g) peeled and finely shredded
daikon
2 jars pickled garlic, 16 oz (500 g) each, drained and
  chopped
1¹/₂ cups (12 fl oz/375 ml) rice vinegar
³/₄ cup (1 oz/30 g) chopped fresh cilantro (coriander)
  roots and stems
7 fresh long red chilies, finely chopped
3¹/₄ cups (28 oz/875 g) granulated (white) sugar
¹/₄ teaspoon salt

In a large saucepan, combine all ingredients and slowly bring to a boil. Reduce heat, then simmer for 20 minutes. Remove from heat and let cool completely. Store in a tightly covered jar in the refrigerator for up to 1 month.

Tips
• To save time, prepare ingredients that require chopping in a food processor.

• This sauce originates from Thailand and it is fast becoming a standard table condiment in the West. Traditionally, it accompanies Thai fish cakes, grilled or fried dishes, and squid (calamari) rings and spring rolls.

Chicken stock

Makes 8 cups (64 fl oz/2 L)

1 chicken, whole, about 2 lb (1 kg)

1 large onion, coarsely sliced

1 large carrot, peeled and chopped

2 celery stalks, chopped

5 fresh cilantro (coriander) stems, including roots

1 teaspoon sea salt

8 black peppercorns

10 cups (80 fl oz/2.5 L) water

In a large saucepan, combine place chicken, onion, carrot, celery, cilantro, salt and peppercorns and cover with water.

Place over medium–high heat and bring liquid to a boil.

Reduce heat to medium–low and simmer for 1–1½ hours, skimming surface occasionally to remove scum and fat.

Remove saucepan from heat. Remove chicken and strain liquid. Allow stock to cool completely, then remove remaining fat from surface.

Tip

To make beef stock, substitute chicken with beef cuts and bones.

Pho beef stock

Makes 8 cups (64 fl oz/2 L)

10 lb (5 kg) beef bones

1 teaspoon sea salt

2-inch (5-cm) piece fresh ginger

3 medium yellow (brown) onions

2 star anise seeds

6 cloves

1 teaspoon black peppercorns

1 cinnamon stick

5 cardamom pods

2 tablespoons fish sauce

Place beef bones in a large stockpot. Cover with cold water, place over high heat and bring to a boil. Boil for 2 minutes. Strain liquid through a large sieve or colander. Discard liquid and keep bones. Return bones to stockpot.

Cover with cold water, add salt and bring to a boil over high heat. Reduce heat to medium–low and simmer for 3–4 hours. While waiting for the water to boil, grill ginger and onions over a gas flame or under a very hot broiler (grill). For ginger, hold with tongs, turn until skin can be easily peeled away, about 3 minutes. For onions, hold each with tongs and turn over flame until skin and outer layer are burnt and slightly soft, 3–4 minutes. Remove and discard burnt outer layer.

Heat a frying pan over high heat and lightly roast anise seeds by swirling them in pan for 2 minutes.

Add ginger, onions, anise seeds and remaining ingredients to simmering stock. After stock has simmered 3–4 hours, strain. Discard solids and skim off any residue.

Use stock immediately for making a pho, or keep, refrigerated and covered, for up to 4 days, or frozen for 1 month.

Coconut cream, milk and water

Choose a good-quality coconut by shaking it to see if it is full of water. If there is none present, discard coconut. If the coconut flesh has spoiled or dried, it will rattle slightly. Hold the coconut in your hand, resting it in a heavy kitchen towel, and use a large knife or small machete to crack coconut by scoring lightly across its circumference. Strike sharply with knife to crack shell. Insert knife blade into the crack to pry apart. Take extra care lest you cut your hand. Alternatively, drop coconut onto a hard concrete surface, or use a hammer.

Use a small hand grater to scrape out coconut meat in shreds. Alternatively, place shells in a moderate oven (350°F/180°C/Gas 4) for 15–20 minutes. The flesh will shrink slightly, facilitating removal. Grate in a food processor.

Put grated coconut in a kitchen towel and wring it tightly or put it in a sieve and press it firmly with the back of a large spoon to extract cream; reserve liquid. A chinois sieve, or China cap, works well here.

Add just enough warm or hot water to cover shredded coconut and press it again to extract thick coconut milk. Repeat again to extract thin coconut milk.

Canned coconut milk or cream can be substituted for fresh. Make sure not to use sweetened coconut milk or cream. Generally speaking, the less the can shakes, the richer the coconut milk. However, just before using, take care not to shake can. Open carefully and spoon off richest portion (refrigeration facilitates this step) to separate it from the thinner coconut milk.

The liquid sloshing inside the coconut is coconut water, not to be confused with its milk or cream. A young coconut with immature flesh holds the greatest volume of coconut water, but only a fully mature coconut should be used for extracting cream or milk from grated meat.

Fish sauce with chilies

Makes about 1½ cups (12 fl oz/375 ml)

1 cup (8 fl oz/250 ml) fish sauce
1 cup (5 oz/150 g) thinly sliced, fresh medium red or
  green chilies
cloves from ½ bulb garlic, finely chopped
2–3 tablespoons fresh lime juice, to taste

In a small bowl or screw-top jar, combine all ingredients,
stir or shake to blend and serve. Refrigerate, covered,
for several days.

Tip

This is the ubiquitous table seasoning of Thailand, used
as commonly as salt and pepper. For a less spicy sauce,
halve chilies lengthwise and scrape away some or all of
the seeds. Then thinly slice chilies as above and
continue.

Chili oil

Makes about 1 cup (8 fl oz/250 ml)

¾ cup (6 fl oz/180 ml) vegetable oil
½ cup dried chili flakes

In a well-ventilated room, heat oil in a wok or small,
heavy saucepan over medium to medium–high heat, just
until surface shimmers. Add chili flakes. Stir briefly and
immediately remove from heat. Let cool. If tightly
covered, chili oil will keep indefinitely at room
temperature.

Chili and coriander dipping sauce

Makes 2 cups (16 fl oz/500 ml)

4 cloves garlic, chopped
1 lemongrass stalk, chopped, or 2 teaspoons grated
  lemon zest (rind)
1 tablespoon chili paste
2 tablespoons fish sauce
1 cup (8 fl oz/250 ml) lemon juice
1 cup (8 fl oz/250 ml) rice wine vinegar
⅓ cup (2 oz/60 g) superfine (caster) sugar
1 teaspoon cornstarch (cornflour) mixed with
  1 tablespoon water
½ cup (⅔ oz/20 g) chopped fresh cilantro (coriander)

In a saucepan over high heat, combine garlic,
lemongrass or lemon zest, chili paste, fish sauce, lemon
juice, vinegar and sugar. Bring to a boil, reduce heat to
low and simmer, covered, to blend flavors, about
10 minutes.

Stir cornstarch and water into sauce, raise heat to
medium and cook, stirring, until sauce is thickened,
2–3 minutes.

Sauce can be stored in airtight container in refrigerator
for up to 7 days.

Right: Fish sauce with chilies; far right: Chili oil

Fish stock

Makes 8 cups (64 fl oz/2 L)

about 2 lb (1 kg) heads and bones of 2 medium-sized
  white-fleshed fish
2 tablespoons light olive oil
1 large onion, coarsely chopped
1 large carrot, peeled and coarsely chopped
2 celery stalks, with leaves, coarsely chopped
3 stems flat-leaf (Italian) parsley
3 stems fresh cilantro (coriander), preferably including
  roots
3 fresh or 6 dried kaffir lime leaves (optional)
8 black peppercorns
1 teaspoon sea salt

Wash fish heads and bones well, removing any gills. Chop
bones so that they fit into a large pot.

In a large pot over high heat, heat oil for 1 minute. Add
fish heads and bones and cook, stirring and turning heads
and bones, until any remaining flesh starts to cook and is
slightly golden, 4–5 minutes.

Add remaining ingredients and stir to combine. Add
enough water to cover bones completely (approximately
8 cups/64 fl oz/2 L) and bring liquid to a steady simmer.
Reduce heat to medium and simmer for 25 minutes. Skim
any scum from surface as stock simmers.

Strain liquid through a very fine sieve. If you don't have a
very fine sieve, line your sieve with a double layer of damp
cheesecloth (muslin). Discard solids.

Allow stock to cool then cover with plastic wrap and
refrigerate if not using immediately.

Vegetable stock

Makes 6 cups (48 fl oz/1.5 L)

2 tablespoons oil
4 large brown onions, unpeeled and chopped
2 large carrots, unpeeled and chopped
2 large parsnips, unpeeled and chopped
5 sticks celery, including leaves, chopped
2 bay leaves
fresh bouquet garni
1 teaspoon whole black peppercorns
12 cups (96 fl oz/3 L) water

Preheat oven to 400ºF (200ºC/Gas 6). In a large baking
dish, heat the oil. Add onion, carrot and parsnip and toss
to coat in oil. Bake until lightly golden, about 30 minutes.

Transfer vegetables to a large heavy-based pan. Add
remaining ingredients and bring to a boil slowly. Reduce
heat and simmer, uncovered, until reduced by half, about
1 hour.

Strain liquid through a very fine sieve. Discard solids.

Allow stock to cool then cover with plastic wrap and
refrigerate if not using immediately.

Tip

Stock can be refrigerated for 2 days. If stored in tightly
covered containers, it can be frozen for 2 months.

Front: Garam masala; back: Penang curry paste

Penang curry paste

Makes about ½ cup (4 fl oz/125 ml)

8 dried red chilies
¼ cup (2 fl oz/60 ml) boiling water
4 scallions (shallots/spring onions)
6 cloves garlic, chopped
2 stalks lemongrass, white part only, chopped
3 fresh cilantro (coriander) roots, coarsely chopped
1 tablespoon peeled and grated fresh ginger
1 teaspoon ground coriander
1 teaspoon ground cumin
2 tablespoons roasted peanuts
2 tablespoons vegetable oil

Put chilies in a small bowl and add boiling water to cover. Let soak for 5 minutes. Drain. Chop chilies coarsely. Transfer to a food processor and add all remaining ingredients. Process to a thick paste. Spoon into a sterilized jar and seal. Store in the refrigerator for up to 3 weeks.

Herb yogurt dip

Serves 8–10 as an accompaniment

1 teaspoon cumin seeds
½ cup (¾ oz/20 g) coarsely chopped fresh mint
½ cup (¾ oz/20 g) coarsely chopped fresh cilantro
  (coriander)
2 teaspoons finely chopped fresh ginger
2 fresh green chilies, coarsely chopped
2½ cups (20 oz/600 g) plain (natural) whole-milk
  yogurt
1 yellow (brown) onion, thinly sliced
salt to taste

In a small saucepan over low heat, dry-roast cumin seeds until fragrant and lightly colored, being careful not to burn. Let cool then grind to a powder in a spice grinder.

In a food processor, combine mint, cilantro, ginger and chili and process until finely chopped.

In a bowl, whisk yogurt. Add onion, ground cumin and chopped herb mixture. Mix well and season with salt. Can be made 2 days ahead. Store in an airtight container in refrigerator.

Garam masala

Makes about ¼ cup (2 fl oz/60 ml)

1 tablespoon cardamom seeds (not pods)
2 cinnamon sticks, broken up
1 teaspoon black peppercorns
1 teaspoon cloves
1 teaspoon cumin seeds
1 teaspoon fennel seeds

In a small skillet, combine all ingredients and stir over medium heat until fragrant, about 1 minute. Transfer to a bowl and let cool. Transfer to a spice or coffee grinder and grind to a fine powder. Store in a tightly sealed jar in a cool, dark place for up to 4 weeks.

Hot chili sauce

Makes 1 cup (8 fl oz/250 ml)

2 lb (1 kg) ripe tomatoes, quartered

3 small dried red chilies, split and seeded

4 tablespoons boiling water

1 tablespoon olive oil

1 onion, finely chopped

1 clove garlic, crushed

olive oil (optional)

Place tomatoes in heavy-bottomed saucepan over low heat and cook stirring occasionally, until they break down and form sauce, about 1 hour. Add a little water if mixture begins to stick. Press through a sieve, set over bowl. (Do not use food processor, as skins need to be removed after tomatoes are cooked.) Set aside.

Place chilies in a bowl, add boiling water and let stand 10 minutes. Remove from water and chop; reserve 1 tablespoon of water. Place chilies and reserved water in food processor and process until smooth. Set aside.

In a frying pan over medium–high heat, warm oil. Add onion and cook until softened, about 2 minutes. Add garlic and cook until aromatic, about 1 minute. Reduce heat to low and stir in chili puree. Add tomato pulp and cook until thickened, about 5 minutes. Remove from heat and allow to cool.

Pour into airtight container and refrigerate until ready to serve. To store for up to 3 weeks, drizzle film of olive oil over top of sauce.

Garlic dipping sauce

Makes ½ cup (4 fl oz/125 ml)

3 tablespoons soy sauce

2 tablespoons Worcestershire sauce

1 tablespoon Asian sesame oil

4 cloves garlic, finely chopped

1 tablespoon superfine (caster) sugar

In a small bowl, combine all ingredients. Stir until sugar dissolves. Cover and chill before serving.

Mango, papaya and green chili relish

Serves 4

1 small ripe mango, peeled, pitted and chopped

¼ small papaya, peeled, seeded and chopped

½ long green chili, seeded and
   finely chopped

6 scallions (shallots/spring onions), sliced

1 fresh kaffir lime leaf, finely shredded, or
   ½ teaspoon grated lime zest (rind)

3 tablespoons fresh lime juice

2 teaspoons Asian sesame oil

In a small bowl, combine mango, papaya, chili, scallions and lime leaf. Stir in lime juice and sesame oil. Mix well.

Cover and chill for 30 minutes.

Nuoc cham nem sauce

Makes about 2 cups (16 fl oz/500 ml)

3 cloves garlic

1 fresh long red chili, seeded

½ cup (4 fl oz/125 ml) fish sauce

¼ cup (2 fl oz/60 ml) rice vinegar or distilled white
   vinegar

⅔ cup (5 fl oz/165 ml) water

3–4 tablespoons sugar to taste

1 carrot, peeled and finely shredded or chopped

½ cup (2 oz/60 g) peeled, shredded and chopped
   green papaya

½ teaspoon ground pepper

In a mortar, pound garlic and chili with a pestle to a paste. Stir in fish sauce, vinegar, water and sugar and continue stirring until sugar is dissolved. Alternatively, in a blender or food processor, combine garlic, chili, fish sauce, vinegar, water and sugar and puree. Stir in shredded carrot, papaya and pepper.

Tips

• This sauce is best consumed on the day it is made or the day after.

• If green papaya is unavailable, substitute peeled, shredded, daikon (giant white radish) or jicama (yam bean). Shredded daikon smells strongly if not used within a few hours.

Massaman curry paste

Makes about ¾ cup (6 fl oz/180 ml)

8 dried long red chilies, seeded

¼ cup (20 g) coriander seeds

2 tablespoons cumin seeds

4 star anise, crushed

2 cinnamon sticks, broken

10 whole cloves

1 teaspoon salt

⅔ cup (5 fl oz/150 ml) vegetable oil

6 large cloves garlic, crushed

2 tablespoons finely chopped shallots (French shallots), preferably pink

6 thin slices galangal, chopped

1 stalk lemongrass, white part only, peeled and chopped

1 teaspoon chopped fresh kaffir lime zest (rind)

Soak dried chilies in warm water for 10 minutes. Drain and pat dry.

In a small frying pan over medium heat, separately toast each spice, stirring constantly, until fragrant. Immediately remove from heat and pour spices into a large mortar or spice grinder. Add salt and grind to a fine powder. Transfer to a small bowl.

In a wok or large, heavy frying pan over medium–high heat, heat oil. Add garlic, shallots and drained chilies. Fry until slightly golden, 1–2 minutes. Remove with a slotted spoon, reserve solids and discard oil.

Place galangal, lemongrass and kaffir lime zest in a large mortar, and pound to a paste, 10–20 minutes. Halfway through, add fried garlic, shallots and chilies and pound until smooth. Add ground spices. Alternatively, grind dried spices; coarsely chop fresh ingredients and place in a food processor then process until finely chopped. If necessary, add a small amount of water, 1 teaspoon at a time.

Tip

Making your own curry paste allows you to vary the ingredients to suit your taste. Tightly covered, fresh curry paste keeps for 3–4 days in the refrigerator. Fried curry paste keeps for two months in the refrigerator or indefinitely in the freezer.

Red curry paste

Makes about 1 cup (8 fl oz/250 ml)

6 red bird's eye or Thai chilies, seeded and
   coarsely chopped
2 teaspoons black peppercorns
2 teaspoons cumin seeds
1 teaspoon sweet paprika
1 teaspoon dried shrimp paste
1 red (Spanish) onion, coarsely chopped
2 stalks lemongrass, white part only, chopped
4 cloves garlic, chopped
1 tablespoon grated fresh galangal
2 tablespoons coarsely chopped fresh cilantro
   (coriander)
2 tablespoons vegetable oil
2 teaspoons fish sauce

In a small skillet, combine chilies, peppercorns, cumin
seeds, paprika and shrimp paste and stir over medium
heat until fragrant, 30–60 seconds. Remove from heat
and let cool. Transfer to a food processor. Add remaining
ingredients and process to a smooth paste. Spoon into
a sterilized jar and seal. Store in refrigerator for up to
3 weeks.

Green curry paste

Makes about 1½ cups (12 fl oz/375 ml)

1 tablespoon coriander seeds
1 tablespoon cumin seeds
4 black peppercorns
1 cup (1⅓ oz/40 g) coarsely chopped fresh cilantro
   (coriander)
2 fresh kaffir lime leaves, shredded
6 cloves garlic, chopped
4 scallions (shallots/spring onions), including green
   parts, coarsely chopped
4 fresh green Thai or Anaheim chilies, seeded and
   coarsely chopped
1 tablespoon grated fresh galangal
1 teaspoon dried shrimp paste
2 stalks lemongrass, white part only, chopped
2 teaspoons fish sauce
2 tablespoons vegetable oil

In a small skillet, combine coriander, cumin seeds and
peppercorns and stir over medium heat until fragrant,
about 1 minute. Empty into a bowl and let cool. Transfer
to a spice or coffee grinder and grind to a fine powder.
Transfer to a food processor and add remaining
ingredients. Process to a smooth paste. Spoon into a
sterilized jar and seal. Store in the refrigerator for up to
3 weeks.

Thai chili dipping sauce

Makes about 1 cup (8 fl oz/250 ml)

15 fresh long green chilies, roasted
1 whole bulb garlic
9 shallots (French shallots), about 3 oz (100 g),
    preferably pink
1/4 teaspoon dried shrimp paste
1/2 teaspoon salt
1 tablespoon fish sauce

Peel and stem roasted chilies but retain seeds. (For a
less piquant sauce, discard some or all of the seeds.)
Preheat oven to 400°F (200°C/Gas 6). Lightly break
unpeeled garlic bulb by pressing on a knife handle with
the heel of your hand, so that the cloves sit loosely
together; do not separate cloves from bulb completely.
Separately wrap the garlic and shallots in aluminum foil.
Roast on top shelf of oven until soft to touch, about
30 minutes. Remove from oven and allow to cool to
touch in foil. Peel shallots and garlic; you should have
about 1/3 cup (1 1/2 oz/45 g) shallots.

In a mortar, pound chilies gently with a pestle to break
them up. Add garlic and pound briefly, then add shallots.
Add shrimp paste and salt and pound again to a coarse
paste. Or, pulse ingredients in a food processor. Stir in
fish sauce. Serve with a selection of vegetable crudités.

Sambal oelek

Makes about 1 1/2 cups (12 fl oz/375 ml)

1 lb (500 g) red chilies
2 1/2 cups (20 fl oz/625 ml) water
1 tablespoon white vinegar
1 teaspoon superfine (caster) sugar
2 tablespoons peanut oil
1/2 cup (4 fl oz/125 ml) boiling water

This mixture of red chilies, vinegar and salt is used
throughout Asian cooking as a flavoring and as a spicy
hot condiment.

Remove stems from chilies. Remove seeds if you want
less fiery sambal oelek. In a saucepan over medium
heat, combine chilies and water and bring to a boil.
Cover, reduce heat to simmer and cook until chilies are
soft, about 15 minutes. Drain. Working in batches, place
chilies in a food processor and process until smooth.
Add vinegar, sugar, peanut oil and boiling water and
process to combine. Pour into sterilized jars, seal and
refrigerate for up to 1 month.

Avocado cream

Makes 1½ cups (12 fl oz/375 ml)

4 oz (125 g) silken tofu, drained
2 teaspoons white (shiro) miso
4 teaspoons white vinegar
1 avocado, peeled, pitted and diced
salt and pepper to taste
1½ tablespoons fresh lime juice
1 teaspoon each finely chopped fresh parsley, chives
   and mint

In a food processor, process tofu until smooth. In a cup, combine 2 tablespoons pureed tofu with miso and stir until smooth. Return tofu mixture to food processor and add all remaining ingredients. Process until well combined.

Tomato salsa with chili and cilantro

Serves 4–6

2 large vine-ripened tomatoes, chopped
1 small red chili, seeded and chopped
½ small red (Spanish) onion, chopped
⅓ cup (½ oz/10 g) chopped fresh cilantro
   (coriander)
2 tablespoons balsamic vinegar
1 tablespoon fresh lime juice
sea salt and freshly ground black pepper

In a bowl, combine tomatoes, chili, onion and cilantro. In a small bowl, combine balsamic vinegar and lime juice, mix well and add to tomato mixture. Stir and season with salt and pepper. Cover and allow to stand at room temperature for 15 minutes before serving.

Tips
• This salsa is excellent with hot-and-spicy money bags, poultry, chili-noodle cakes and shrimp (prawns). It also makes a delicious accompaniment for fried wontons and grilled fish or chicken.

• Bird's eye or serrano chilies are recommended for this recipe.

Glossary

Almonds: The nut of the almond tree. Available without shells, blanched, whole, flaked or slithered.

Anchovy paste: A thick, Western sauce made from pounded salted anchovies. Available in tubes in supermarkets and specialty food stores.

Arborio rice: A type of short-grain rice traditionally grown in Italy and used to make risotto. The high starch content of arborio rice gives risotto its characteristic creamy texture.

Asafoetida: Grinding the dried resinous gum of a giant fennel plant produces this foul-smelling yellow powder. Its unappealing aroma disappears when it is added in small amounts to food, offering a mild onion or garlic flavor—a fact that caught the attention of the Hindu Brahmins and Jains in India, whose diets do not allow the use of onions and garlic. It is also added to help prevent the gastric distress associated with eating lentils and beans along with other foods high in fiber.

Asian sesame oil: Rich, dark- or golden-colored oil extracted from sesame seeds. Oil made from toasted seeds has a pronounced nutty flavor.

Asian chili sauce:(tuong ot) Asian chili sauces, such as Vietnamese or Thai, are slightly thick, bright orange-red in color, and made with crushed chilies, vinegar, garlic and sugar.

Atta flour: A fine wholemeal flour made from low gluten, soft-textured wheat. Also known as chapati flour. Sold in Indian stores.

Bamboo leaves: Long, narrow leaves available dried from Asian food stores. Leaves impart subtle flavor to food, but are not eaten. Soak briefly in boiling water to soften before use.

Bamboo shoots: Young shoots of a tropical plant, which are boiled to retain their sweet flavor. Most commonly found canned, packed in water.

Banana leaves: Large leaves from the banana plant, used to line bamboo steamers or for wrapping foods prior to steaming. Parchment (baking) paper may be substituted. The leaves are available fresh or frozen.

Bean sprouts: Sprouted beans and peas add a fresh flavor and crunchy texture to salads and other Asian dishes. Mung bean sprouts are sold fresh or canned. Snow pea (mange-tout) sprouts are available fresh. Fresh sprouts are preferred for their clean taste and crisp texture; store in refrigerator for up to 3 days.

Besan flour: A pale yellow flour made from chickpeas. Available from health food stores.

Burghul: See Cracked wheat

Bok choy: Asian variety of cabbage with dark green leaves and thick white stems. Sizes vary from baby bok choy, about 6 inches (15 cm) long, to bok choy as long as a celery stalk.

Cellophane noodles: Thin translucent dried noodles made from mung-bean starch and sold in bundles. Also called bean thread noodles.

Chat masala: Sometimes called chaat masala, this tasty, tart mixture of toasted and ground spices and other flavorings is sprinkled over food just before serving. It may contain any of the following ingredients: black salt, table salt, asafoetida, cumin, coriander, dried mint, ginger, mace, garam masala, pomegranate seeds, chilies, black pepper and amchur powder (ground dried green mango).

Chili oil: Spicy oil produced by steeping red chilies in oil. It is available bottled or you can prepare your own (see page 220).

Chili paste: Fiery condiment made from ground red chilies and sometimes garlic. Use in small quantities.

Chilies: As a general rule, the smaller the chili the hotter it is. For a milder taste, remove the seeds and membrane of chili before adding to dishes. Dried chili flakes and chili powder can be substituted.

Chinese barbecue pork: Fatty, boneless pork that has been marinated and roasted. Sold sliced or whole in Chinese markets and used in stir-fries and other dishes. Store up to 2 days in refrigerator.

Chinese broccoli: Broccoli with white flowers and a bitter taste. Also known as gai laan. Sometimes confused with choy sum. Chinese broccoli and choy sum can be used in place of each other.

Chinese (napa) cabbage: Milder in flavor than regular cabbage. Cook for a minimum of time to retain crunchy texture or use whole leaves to wrap food.

Chinese dried mushrooms: Intensely flavorful, dark mushrooms that need to be rehydrated before use. The stems are discarded. Flavorful fresh mushrooms make an acceptable substitute.

Chinese five spice powder: This is made of an equal mixture of ground Szechuan peppercorns, star anise, fennel, cloves and cinnamon. Available at most supermarkets.

Chinese powdered red food coloring: A deep red powder, traditionally used to color Chinese barbecued pork. Sold as a food coloring and is available from Asian supermarkets. Use in small quantities. Add to marinades to color food prior to cooking.

Chinese roasted duck: Sold freshly roasted in Chinese markets, these ducks are seasoned and glazed before roasting to yield moist, flavorful meat. Use 1–2 days after purchase. Roasted chicken may be substituted.

Choy sum: Also known as flowering cabbage, this mild-flavored Chinese green has thin stalks bearing leaves and yellow flowers, all of which are used in cooking.

Cilantro: Pungent, fragrant leaves from the coriander plant, resembling parsley and also called Chinese parsley as well as fresh coriander. Coriander roots are also used.

Coconut milk and cream: These are made from grated coconut flesh (not the liquid inside coconuts). Thicker coconut cream adds more flavor than the thinner coconut milk. Available in cans from supermarkets.

Coconut vinegar: Sweet tasting, cloudy white vinegar made from coconuts and sold in bottles in Asian markets.

Comino: See Cumin.

Coriander: The tiny yellow-tan seeds of the cilantro (coriander) plant. Used whole or ground as a spice.

Cracked wheat: The whole wheat berry broken into coarse, medium or fine particles. Also called burghul.

Cumin: Also known as comino. The small crescent-shaped seeds have an earthy, nutty flavor. Available whole or ground.

Curry paste: Condiment consisting of curry seasonings and red or green chilies. Both red and green curry pastes are available bottled or you may make your own versions (see page 227).

Daikon: A long, thick "giant" white radish, principally associated with Japan. Choose a firm, crisp specimen and peel before using.

Dashi: Japanese fish broth made from dried bonito fish flakes (katsuobushi) and konbu/kombu (a seaweed). Available in concentrated liquid, powder or dried granules from Asian food stores. Combine with water to the required consistency. Substitute other stocks.

Egg noodles: Used extensively in Asian cooking, these noodles are available fresh or dried in a variety of widths: thin, round or flat.

Fenugreek: The seed of an aromatic plant of the pea family, native to the Mediterranean region. Has a bittersweet, burnt sugar aftertaste, available whole or ground.

Fish sauce: Also known as nam pla, nuoc nam and patis, this distinctive, salty sauce is made from fermented shrimp or fish and is used similarly to soy sauce to enhance and balance the flavor of dishes. Some are much saltier than others; use sparingly and add to taste.

Five spice powder: A mixture of five spices of equal parts—cinnamon, cloves, fennel seed, star anise and szechuan pepper.

Flat-leaf parsley: Parsley with a flat leaf and stronger flavor than curly-leaf parsley. Also known as Italian or Continental parsley. Fresh parsley can be stored for up to 1 week in a plastic bag in the refrigerator.

Flowering cabbage: See Choy sum.

Fried onion: Crisp, deep-fried onion sold in packages in Asian markets.

Garam masala: A blend of spices, cardamom, cumin, coriander, cinnamon, cloves and pepper. Store away from sunlight. (See page 223 for recipe.)

Ghee: A form of clarified fat or pure butter fat, originating in Indian. Has a high smoke point and nutty, caramel-like flavor.

Ginger: Thick rootlike rhizome of the ginger plant, with a sharp, pungent flavor. Once the thin tan skin is peeled away from fresh ginger, the flesh is grated and used in sauces, marinades, stir-fries and dressings, or is sliced, bruised and added to stocks and soups. Store fresh ginger in the refrigerator for 2–3 days.

Glacé (cooking) ginger: Diced fresh ginger cooked in a sugar syrup. Available from supermarkets.

Glutinous rice: Generally white and sometimes dark rice that cooks to a sticky mass rather than separate grains. Also called sticky rice.

Green papaya: Unripe papaya used grated in Asian cooking. Because it is very sticky, oil your hands or wear gloves and oil the grater before preparing.

Hoisin sauce: Sweet, thick sauce made from soybeans and also containing vinegar, sugar, chilies and other seasonings. Bottled hoisin sauce can be stored indefinitely in the refrigerator.

Hokkien noodles: Fat, round, thick wheat noodles, usually dark yellow and available fresh from Asian stores.

Hot bean paste: Hot, thick, red-brown sauce made from fermented soybeans, chilies, garlic and spices. Sometimes called red bean paste or chili bean paste.

Jasmine rice: Aromatic long-grain rice popular in Thai cooking.

Jicama (yam bean): Also known as sweet turnip. Has crunchy and slightly sweet flesh. Peel before use in stir-fries. Available fresh from Asian food stores. Water chestnuts can be substituted.

Kaffir lime: The distinctive fragrant double leaves and fruit of this Asian tree are increasingly available fresh from Asian and many Western supermarkets. Frozen and dried leaves and frozen fruit are also available but lack the flavor of the fresh.

Ketjap manis: Also known as kecap manis, this thick Indonesian soy sauce is sweetened with palm sugar. Available in sweet or semi-sweet varieties, it is versatile and especially suitable for use with tempeh, to brush on deep-fried tofu and in stir-fries.

Korean watercress: Similar to the watercress found in most supermarkets, the Korean variety has a more pungent taste. Only the stems are used in the recipes.

Krachai (Chinese keys): A long, thin rhizome with a subtle, almost medicinal flavor. Krachai is often mistaken for lesser galangal, which is different in taste and appearance. Also called "lesser ginger." Not commonly available fresh, except in Asia. Bottled or pickled krachai tastes insipid by comparison. Simply omit if unavailable.

Lemongrass: A popular lemon-scented grass used in Asian-style dishes. Use only the white part or the bulb. Trim the root and remove the outer layer. Chop finely or bruise by hitting with a meat mallet or blunt side of a chef's knife to bring out the flavor.

Long bean: Related to the black-eyed pea, this thin, flexible but crisp-textured green bean is cut into short lengths before cooking. Long beans are also called snake beans and yard-long beans, though most found in markets are 24 inches (60 cm) or less in length.

Lotus root: A root vegetable that can be stuffed or sliced and added to stir-fries for a crunchy texture.

Available frozen, canned and sometimes fresh from Asian food stores. Scrape fresh lotus root and soak in water with a dash of vinegar or lemon juice to stop discoloration. Water chestnuts or jicama (yam bean) can be substituted.

Massaman curry paste: A mild curry paste with a hint of cinnamon, nutmeg and cloves. Not as hot as green or red curry paste.

Mirin: A sweet Japanese rice wine used for cooking. Sweet sherry can be substituted.

Miso: Thick paste of fermented ground soybeans, used in Japanese soups and other dishes. Light-colored varieties of miso are milder in flavor than dark-colored pastes.

Mizuna: A feathery Japanese salad green with a delicate flavor.

Nam pla: See Fish sauce.

Oyster mushrooms: Creamy white mushrooms with fanshaped caps, named for their resemblance to an oyster. Possessing a very mild, delicate flavor, oyster mushrooms grow in the wild and are cultivated. Available fresh in well stocked supermarkets and produce markets. Substitute button mushrooms if unavailable.

Oyster sauce: Thick, dark brown Chinese sauce made from fermented dried oysters and soy sauce, and sold in bottles. It is used to add a mild or intense briny flavor to stir-fries and other dishes.

Palm sugar: The sap of the palm tree, reduced to a moist sugar. Popular in Asian cuisine. The darker the color, the more caramel the flavor. Brown sugar can be substituted. Available in wrapped blocks or jars. Thinly shave sugar off blocks with a knife or vegetable peeler. Keep the lid on jars tightly or the sugar can dry out.

Paprika: A blend of dried red-skinned chilies. The flavor can range from slightly sweet and mild to pungent and hot.

Pink pickled ginger and red pickled ginger: Fresh ginger thinly sliced or shredded and pickled in sweet vinegar. Red ginger (gari) is slightly saltier than pink (beni shoga). Traditionally accompanies sushi and sashimi.

Available in jars and packets from Asian food stores and some supermarkets.

Preserved lemons: Lemons preserved in a mixture of salt and lemon juice and sometimes spices for about a month. Distinctive flavor popular in Moroccan cooking. Pulp can be used but is usually discarded and only the zest (rind) is used.

Rice: A wide variety of rice is used in Asian cooking. Glutinous rice types, sometimes called sticky rices for their consistency, have a high percentage of gluten. These short- or long-grain varieties are often used in desserts. Nonglutinous rice types, with their lower gluten content, cook to form separate, fluffy grains and are used to accompany curries and other Asian dishes. Jasmine rice is a nonglutinous, long-grain Thai variety known for its appealing fragrance and taste.

Rice paper wrappers: Flavorless, edible, transparent wrappers used to wrap food to be eaten as is or deep-fried. Available square or round and in large and small sizes in Asian food stores.

Rice vinegar: A mild vinegar made from rice. Used to make sushi vinegar. Substitute distilled cider vinegar, but dilute with a little water as flavor is too strong.

Rice wine: Sweet, low-alcohol Chinese wine, also known as shaoxing wine, made from fermented glutinous rice. Sake or dry sherry can be substituted.

Sake: A dry Japanese rice wine used for cooking. Not the same as sake for drinking. Dry sherry or Chinese cooking wine can be substituted.

Sambal oelek: Indonesian paste consisting of ground chilies combined with salt and occasionally vinegar. This spicy condiment is available bottled or you can prepare your own (see page 228).

Shaoxing wine: See rice wine.

Shichimi (Seven spices): Also known as shichimi togarashi and seven-spice seasoning, this peppery Japanese condiment is made up of seven different seasonings: red chili flakes (togarashi), white sesame seeds, nori (seaweed) flakes, sansho (Japanese prickly ash berries), white poppy seeds, black hemp seeds and dried mandarin orange peel. Available in small jars from Asian food stores.

Shiitake mushrooms: Also known as Chinese black mushrooms. Available fresh and dried from supermarkets and Asian food stores. Dried shiitake, which have a much stronger flavor than fresh, should be soaked in warm water for 20 minutes to soften. Stem both fresh and dried shiitake before use.

Shrimp paste: Produced by drying, salting and pounding shrimp into a pungent-flavored paste that is then formed into blocks or cakes.

Soy sauce: Salty sauce made from soybeans and used both as an ingredient and as a table condiment. Dark soy sauce, usually used in cooking, is thicker and often less salty than light soy sauce, which is added to dipping sauces. Low-sodium products are also available.

Star anise: The dried eight-pointed star-shaped seed pod of a tree belonging to the magnolia family. Star anise is one of the ingredients of Chinese five spice powder. It is also used whole, in segments or ground in Asian cooking. It has an intense liquorice flavor.

Sweet chili sauce: Use as a dipping sauce or combine with other sauces, such as soy, plum or ketjap manis. May also contain garlic and/or ginger. Hotter and less-sweet chili sauces may be substituted.

Tahini (sesame paste): A smooth paste made from ground sesame seeds. Some are thicker than others, so add extra water if required. Available from most supermarkets.

Tamarind: Available as powder, paste or pulp, this popular Asian fruit adds a sour flavor. Soak required amount of pulp in hot water for about 15 minutes, then push through a fine-mesh sieve to extract the liquid, discarding the pulp. Dissolve powders and pastes before use, but be aware that some can be quite salty.

Thai sweet chili sauce: Mild chili sauce with a sweet aftertaste, used to flavor dishes during cooking and often as a dipping sauce.

Tikka masala curry paste: A mild curry paste. Other curry pastes can be substituted.

Tofu: Produced from soybeans that have been dried, soaked, cooked, pureed and pressed to form cakes or squares that range in texture from soft to firm. Mild in flavor, tofu readily absorbs the seasonings of the preparations in which it is used.

Turmeric: A dried, powdery spice produced from the rhizome of a tropical plant related to ginger. It has a strong, spicy flavor and yellow color. Also known as Indian saffron.

Udon noodles: Soft, pale Japanese noodles made from wheat and available fresh or dried and in several widths.

Vermicelli noodles: Very thin noodles made of rice flour. Sometimes referred to as cellophane noodles. Available dried in Asian food stores and supermarkets.

Wasabi: Very hot, Japanese green horseradish, traditionally served with sushi and sashimi. Available ready to use in tubes and as powder that is mixed with water but only as required as pungency is easily lost. Occasionally available fresh; peel and finely grate in a circular motion.

Water chestnut: Tuber of a plant grown in Asia, round in shape with subtle sweet, crunchy, light-colored flesh. Water chestnuts are widely available canned. After opening, store in clean water in the refrigerator for up to 3 weeks.

Wonton wrapper: Thin sheets of wheat- or egg-based dough, circular or square in shape, used to enclose a variety of fillings. They are available fresh or frozen.

Index

Guide to weights & measures

The conversions given in the recipes in this book are approximate. Whichever system you use, remember to follow it consistently, thereby ensuring that the proportions are consistent throughout a recipe.

Weights

Imperial	Metric
$\frac{1}{3}$ oz	10 g
$\frac{1}{2}$ oz	15 g
$\frac{3}{4}$ oz	20 g
1 oz	30 g
2 oz	60 g
3 oz	90 g
4 oz ($\frac{1}{4}$ lb)	125 g
5 oz ($\frac{1}{3}$ lb)	150 g
6 oz	180 g
7 oz	220 g
8 oz ($\frac{1}{2}$ lb)	250 g
9 oz	280 g
10 oz	300 g
11 oz	330 g
12 oz ($\frac{3}{4}$ lb)	375 g
16 oz (1 lb)	500 g
2 lb	1 kg
3 lb	1.5 kg
4 lb	2 kg

Volume

Imperial	Metric	Cup
1 fl oz	30 ml	
2 fl oz	60 ml	$\frac{1}{4}$
3 fl oz	90 ml	$\frac{1}{3}$
4 fl oz	125 ml	$\frac{1}{2}$
5 fl oz	150 ml	$\frac{2}{3}$
6 fl oz	180 ml	$\frac{3}{4}$
8 fl oz	250 ml	1
10 fl oz	300 ml	$1\frac{1}{4}$
12 fl oz	375 ml	$1\frac{1}{2}$
13 fl oz	400 ml	$1\frac{2}{3}$
14 fl oz	440 ml	$1\frac{3}{4}$
16 fl oz	500 ml	2
24 fl oz	750 ml	3
32 fl oz	1L	4

Oven temperature guide

The Celsius (°C) and Fahrenheit (°F) temperatures in this chart apply to most electric ovens. Decrease by 25°F or 10°C for a gas oven or refer to the manufacturer's temperature guide. For temperatures below 325°F (160°C), do not decrease the given temperature.

Oven description	°C	°F	Gas Mark
Cool	110	225	$\frac{1}{4}$
	130	250	$\frac{1}{2}$
Very slow	140	275	1
	150	300	2
Slow	170	325	3
Moderate	180	350	4
	190	375	5
Moderately Hot	200	400	6
Fairly Hot	220	425	7
Hot	230	450	8
Very Hot	240	475	9
Extremely Hot	250	500	10

Useful conversions

$\frac{1}{4}$ teaspoon	1.25 ml
$\frac{1}{2}$ teaspoon	2.5 ml
1 teaspoon	5 ml
1 Australian tablespoon	20 ml (4 teaspoons)
1 UK/US tablespoon	15 ml (3 teaspoons)

Butter/Shortening

1 tablespoon	$\frac{1}{2}$ oz	15 g
$1\frac{1}{2}$ tablespoons	$\frac{3}{4}$ oz	20 g
2 tablespoons	1 oz	30 g
3 tablespoons	$1\frac{1}{2}$ oz	45 g

Published in the United States in 2007 by Periplus Editions (HK) Ltd., with editorial offices at 364 Innovation Drive, North Clarendon, Vermont 05759 U.S.A.. and 130 Joo Seng Road #06-01, Singapore 368357.

ISBN-10: 0-7946-5035-X
ISBN-13: 978-0-7946-5035-3

Published by Lansdowne Publishing Pty Ltd
Level 1, 18 Argyle St, Sydney NSW 2000, Australia
www.lansdownepublishing.com.au

Text: Katharine Blakemore, Robert Carmack, Soon Young Choong, Didier Corlou, Bettina Jenkins,
   Ajoy Joshi, Vicki Liley, Sompon Nabnian, Jacki Passmore, Jan Purser, Suzie Smith, Brigid Treloar,
   Nguyen Thanh Van, Rosemary Wadey
Design: Grant Slaney, The Modern Art Production Group
Photography: Quentin Bacon, Alan Benson, Ben Dearnley, Andrew Elton, Chris Jones, Vicky Liley,
   Louise Lister, Andre Martin
Editor: Joanne Holliman
Production Manager: Sally Stokes
Project Co-ordinator: Kate Merrifield

Distributed by

North America, Latin America
& Europe
Tuttle Publishing
364 Innovation Drive
North Clarendon,
VT 05759-9436 U.S.A.
Tel: 1 (802) 773-8930
Fax: 1 (802) 773-6993
info@tuttlepublishing.com
www.tuttlepublishing.com

Japan
Tuttle Publishing
Yaekari Building, 3rd Floor
5-4-12 Osaki, Shinagawa-ku
Tokyo 141-0032
Tel: (81) 3 5437-0171
Fax: (81) 3 5437-0755
tuttle-sales@gol.com

Asia Pacific
Berkeley Books Pte. Ltd.
130 Joo Seng Road
#06-01 Singapore 368357
Tel: (65) 6280-1330
Fax: (65) 6280-6290
inquiries@periplus.com.sg
www.periplus.com

10 09 08 07
8 7 6 5 4 3 2 1

Set in Helvetica on QuarkXPress
Printed in Singapore